Sunset
CRAFTS for
CHILDREN

By the Sunset Editorial Staff
Book Editor: Marian May

Lane Books · Menlo Park, California

FOREWORD

Several years ago Sunset published a craft book for adults entitled Things to Make for Children. Since then numerous parents and teachers have requested a companion book—a collection of craft projects that children themselves could make. Sunset's editors feel that, in this age of super speed and mechanization, all people, perhaps children especially, need to satisfy the urge to create. So, in keeping with this idea, Crafts for Children has been outfitted with nearly two hundred projects, mainly for children from 5 to 12, but with some projects that will appeal to older boys and girls, too. As with all Sunset craft books, the reader is taught how to make objects, but he is also urged to create his own designs.

In preparing Crafts for Children, Marian May, crafts writer and editor, and Beryl Foote, artist and teacher, conferred frequently with art teachers and leaders of children's groups. They reviewed stacks of art work, designed projects and guided children in creating them, and organized the finished material for use in this book. Certain of the projects were selected from recent issues of Sunset magazine.

ACKNOWLEDGMENTS

Our thanks to the following who contributed advice and designs: Ann Bowns, Madeleine Christenson, Sherry Gellner, Jean Groberg, Clark Henley, Louis Hicks, Mary Keller, Julia Majdrakoff, Karl Mann, Carole McCarty, Patricia McLaren, Ann Middleton, Kay Nation, Eleanor Van Rensselaer, William J. Shelley, Phyllis Strasser, Roberta Winbigler. Also, our special appreciation to Deborah Neve for the drawings throughout the book.

Nearly all of the projects are child-tested—made by a panel of special contributors that was happily non-expert, just boys and girls with ordinary interest in "making something." They are: Jeanette Armstrong, Audrienne Armstrong, Andy Clark, Susie Clark, Tracy Cox, David Favis, Jennifer Foote, Michael Foote, Darrell Fort, Keith Fort, Grant Groberg, Linda Groberg, Laurie Grys, Peter Hicks, Alan May, Nancy May, Holly McDowell, Cindy Monroe, Tracy Monroe, Danny Pesch, Dana Priest, Terra Smith, Robin Zaft.

COVER PHOTOGRAPH by Jack McDowell

Executive Editor, Sunset Books: David E. Clark

Tenth Printing February 1973

CONTENTS

Pencils and Crayons; Chalk and Paints; Finger Painting; Dip and Dye; Printing with Sponges, Erasers, Inner Tubes, Odds and Ends; Monoprints; Block Prints; Notebooks and Folders; Torn Paper Pictures; Tissue Paper Flowers; Pinwheels; Weaving; Paper Chains; Cylinder Figures; Greeting Cards; Ornaments and Decorations; Pins and Beads; Pencil Holder; Owl Bank; Papier Mache Zoo; Fancy Paper Bags; Snowman Mobile

Decorated Tags and Note Paper; Bookends; Bookmarks; "Paper" Doll and Dresses; Cloth Scrap Picture; Embroidery Stitch Chart; Stitchery Pictures and Wall Hangings; Pincushions; Easy Weaving; Batik; Spray Paint Stencils; Iron-On Designs; Felt Pen and Crayon Designs

Nail Picture; House Sign; Wood and Paper Pictures; Collection Displays; Tic-Tac-Toe Board; Pencil Holder; Stilts; Balsa Wood Constructions; Kites

Ceramic Pendants and Animal Mobiles; Candleholders; Big Bug Paperweight; Clay-Dough Decorations; Mosaic Hot Pad and Pictures; Junk Mosaic; Flower Pot Rim; Seed Mosaics; Plaster Prints; Sand Casts

Souvenir Rubbings; Decorating Rocks; Leaves on Letters; Printing with Pods; Displaying Leaf Collections; Teasel Flowers; Yule Log; Walking Sticks; Driftwood Zoo and Sculpture; Woven Nature Collection

Paper Bag Puppets and Turkey; Paper Plate Music; Paper Plate Elephant Mask; Funny Eyes; Egg Carton Witches and Candleholder; "Boo" Mask; Long Tape Greeting Cards; Newspaper Necklace; Old-Fashioned Valentines; Easter Eggs; Mobile with Walnut Boats; Walking Walnut Animals; Paper Flowers; Tin Can Lanterns; Double Candles; Mexican Yarn Ornaments; Wax Paper Mobile; Decorated Bottles; Toothpick Stars

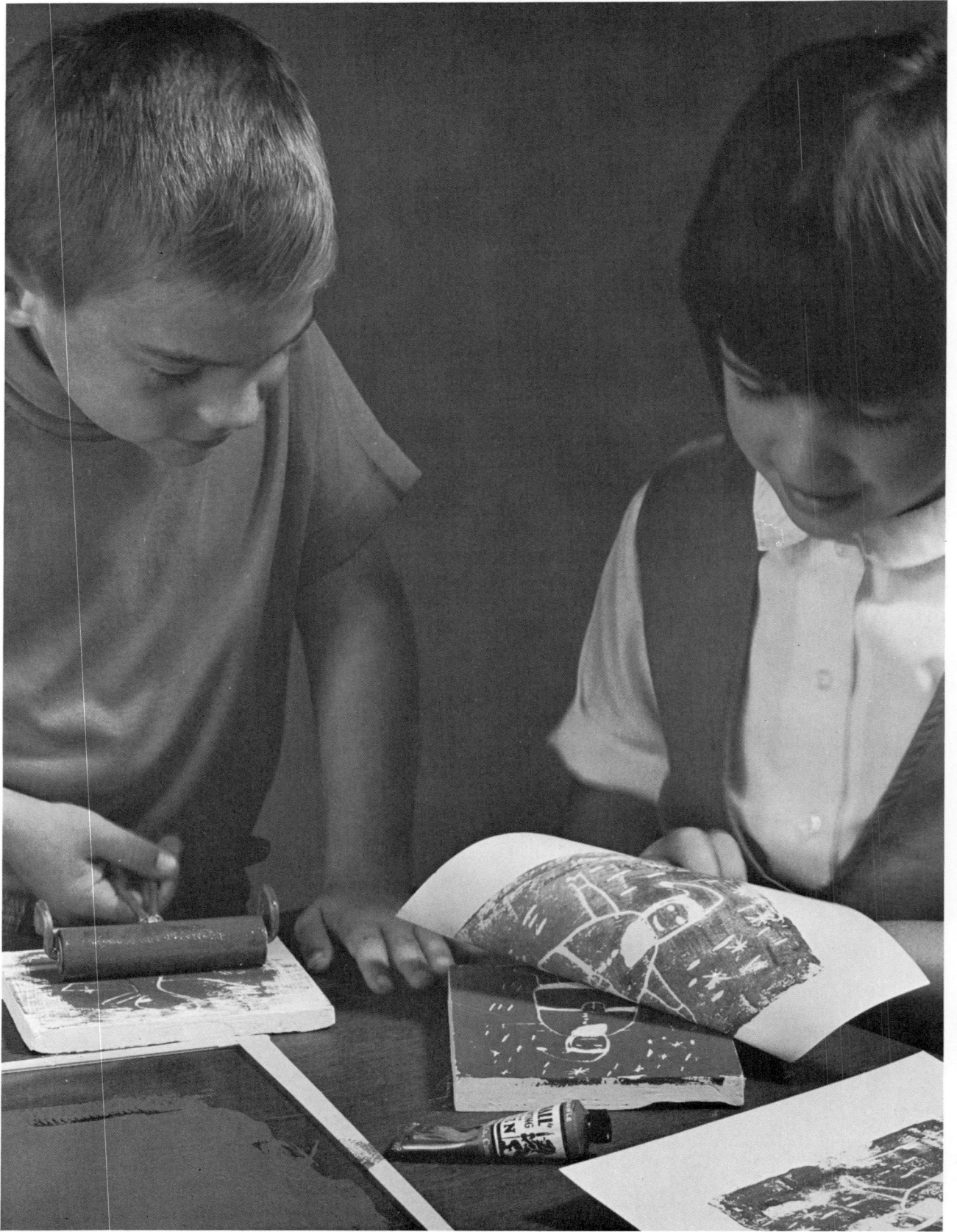

NOTES TO PARENTS

Children seem to be naturally filled with a desire for "something to do," and there is probably no child who is not pleased when the "something to do" involves being creative. Although much of today's highly passive entertainment—television, movies, spectator sports—fills certain needs, it does not always answer the need to create. Aimed not just at children who have artistic talents and who seek out craft projects on their own, this book is based on the belief that all children like to create using their hands.

The projects shown cover many kinds of handicrafts that will appeal to children from about 5 to 12 years of age. They encourage a youngster to make things out of other things, either on his own or with a minimum of direction. Many of the projects are especially good for groups of children and adapt well to short sessions with Scouts, Camp Fire Girls, or day campers.

Any emphasis on paper crafts is intentional. Paper is one of the first materials children learn to use; it is inexpensive and readily available in a variety of forms. Also covered in this book are elementary woodworking, stitchery, ceramics, and mosaics. There are suggestions for projects that can be made while on vacation and with souvenirs brought home. There is a variety of projects which make use of discards such as plastic bottles, newspapers, or tin cans.

The paints, brushes, and other equipment called for can be purchased at a variety store or an art supply store. Many of the other materials can be found right in the home.

Notice that the instructions are addressed to the child. The names of materials and tools are printed in boldface type so that they can be easily seen. The child is also reminded to protect his work table with newspapers or plastic and is encouraged to form good habits in keeping both his equipment and himself clean.

Most children will enjoy their handiwork for a long time, and they are pleased when it is accepted as part of the home decoration. Consequently, an attempt has been made to suggest projects that the parent, as well as the child, will be able to treasure.

The children shown on the opposite page are making prints using a plaster block. Detailed instructions for this project are given on page 69.

HOW TO START

Get yourself ready

One of the most important things to do before you begin a project is to make sure your hands are clean. A smudge from dirty fingers will ruin a new piece of paper, cloth, or balsa wood before you even get started. It is also important to wear a smock to keep your clothes clean. An old, large shirt buttoned up the back works well. Ask your mother to cut off the sleeves to fit your arms.

Get your work place ready

Get together whatever you need **before** you start a project. If you are going to use pencils or crayons you will need a smooth, clean table. If the table is rough, place your drawing paper on a thick magazine so the lines you draw will be clear. When you paint, cover the table with newspapers or a piece of thin plastic. Water used for dipping your brushes should be kept in a container that isn't easily knocked over.

... AND FINISH

Clean up your work place

If you have been painting, carefully wash your brushes and tightly screw lids and caps on paint jars and tubes. Never leave crayons in a place where the sun or heat will melt them. Put away all scraps of paper, cloth, wood, or other materials you have been using. A big shoe box makes a good container for your craft materials. The box can be decorated in one of the ways shown in this book.

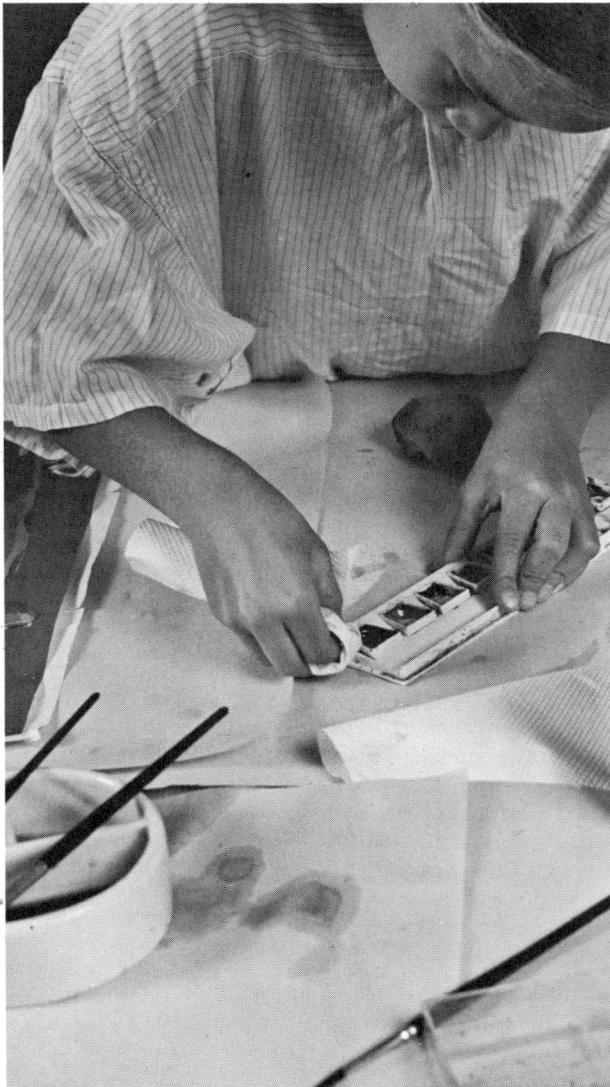

Clean up yourself

After you have cleaned your work place—wiped up drops of paint and cleaned brushes, swept up sawdust and scraps of paper—be sure that you clean up yourself, too. Wash your hands well so you won't smudge your finished project. Scrub off any paint or glue that has dropped on you or your clothing. Then hang up your work shirt or smock so that it will be handy when you are ready to start again.

PAPER CRAFTS

PENCILS & CRAYONS • CHALK & PAINTS • FINGER PAINTING • DIP & DYE
PRINTING WITH SPONGES, ERASERS, INNER TUBES, ODDS & ENDS
MONOPRINTS • BLOCK PRINTS • NOTEBOOKS & FOLDERS • TORN PAPER PICTURES
TISSUE PAPER FLOWERS • PINWHEELS • WEAVING • PAPER CHAINS
CYLINDER FIGURES • GREETING CARDS • ORNAMENTS & DECORATIONS
PINS & BEADS • PENCIL HOLDER • OWL BANK • PAPIER MACHE ZOO
FANCY PAPER BAGS • SNOWMAN MOBILE • LADYBUG TABLE SETTING

Paper is the most common craft material we have. You can paint, draw or color on paper. You can dip it in paint or stamp on designs. You can fold it, tear it, cut it, or make papier mache. Here are some of the materials you may need for making the paper crafts shown in this chapter.

Paper. Brightly colored construction paper and white drawing paper are used in many of the projects. Other crafts call for heavier poster paper or cardboard, colorful tissue paper, and crepe paper. To make papier mache projects, you will need old newspapers or paper towels (white towels are the best). Newsprint is good to use for big drawings or paintings. Sometimes you can get ends of rolls at a newspaper office. Thin typing paper is handy for tracing and carbon paper will transfer your drawing to another paper.

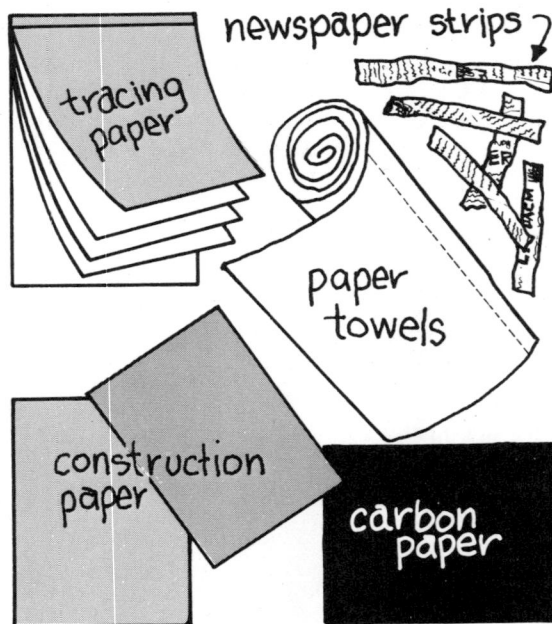

Pencils. The best pencils for drawing are those marked "Drawing" or "Soft Lead." Keep them sharpened and in a container like the papier mache elephant on page 31 or the wooden holder on page 51. Colored pencils come in all colors and may be bought in sets or one by one.

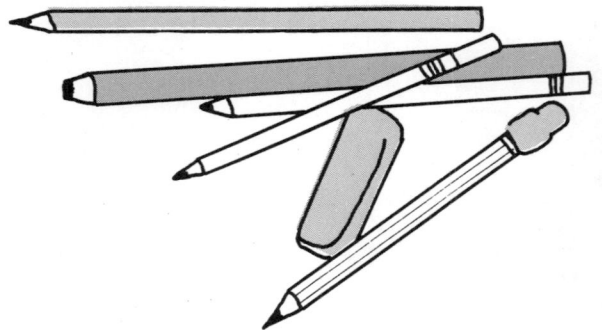

Crayons. One of the easiest ways to make color designs on paper is to use crayons. They come in every color you can imagine. If a crayon breaks, you can tape the pieces together with sticky backed tape. Used pieces that are too short for drawing can be used for crayon rubbings and other crafts. Warning: keep crayons away from sun and heat.

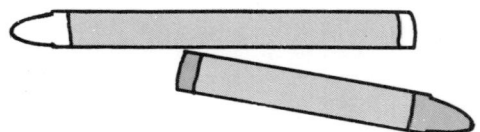

Marking pens. Felt or nylon tipped marking pens come in many bright colors and many sizes. They are very handy for making posters and printing on book covers. Because the ink in the pens will fade and dry out, be sure to keep them capped when you are not using them.

felt tipped pen

Paint. Some of the projects shown in this chapter use a water-based paint (this means that the paint has been mixed with water and can be cleaned up with water). **Acrylic paints** are also water-based and come in jars or tubes of bright colors. Because acrylics dry fast, be sure to clean your brushes right after using them. The acrylics give a dull finish. For a shiny finish, use polymer medium. This glaze comes in a jar, is colorless, and is brushed on over the acrylic paint. **Poster paint** or **tempera** are colorful paints that can be bought ready mixed in jars. You can also buy them in powder form to be mixed with water until creamy-thick. **Water colors** come in little cakes or tubes. They can be used for painting pictures or as a wash (a thin, watered-down coat sometimes painted over finished drawings and paintings). Page 13 for an example of a wash. **Block printing paint** can be either water- or oil-based. Although poster paints and acrylics can be used for some printing projects, regular block printing paint works the best.

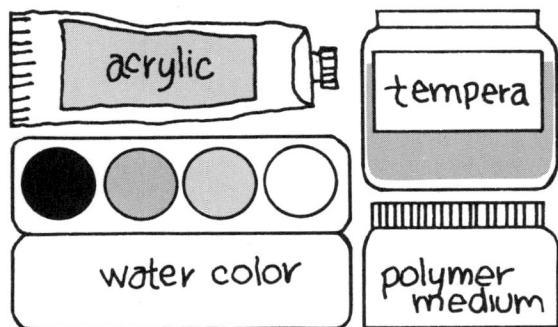
acrylic
tempera
water color
polymer medium

Brushes. Paint brushes come in all sizes. They are also available in different shapes. Clean your brushes after each use. If you have used a water-based paint, clean your brushes with water. Use turpentine if you have used oil paints. Store the brushes flat; never leave them in the paint jar.

Glue, paste, and tape. Rubber cement is excellent for gluing together paper, but white library paste also works well. The best all-round glue (not only for paper, but for cloth, wood, and plastic) is household white glue. When a special glue is needed to make a project, the directions will tell you. Sticky backed tape has many uses and comes in colors or is clear.

glue
tape
paste
rubber cement

Scissors and craft knives. For young children, scissors should have rounded points. A craft knife—necessary for some projects—has removable blades that fit into the handle. Most art stores sell them. Do all cutting with a knife on a pad of newspapers or heavy cardboard.

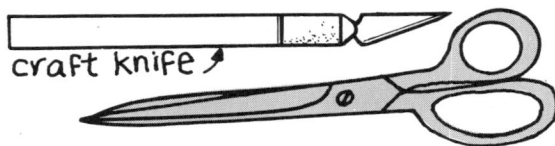
craft knife

Other equipment. A ruler, stapler, paper punch, and compass for making circles are all handy when you are working on paper projects. A cooky sheet or piece of glass and a brayer (roller) are needed when you make mono or block prints. Use an old muffin tin or aluminum pie pan for mixing the paint.

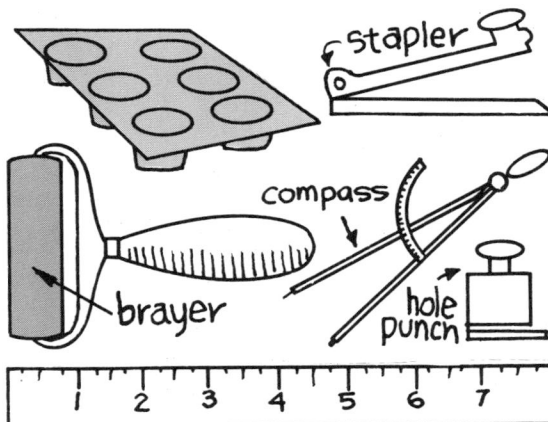
stapler
compass
brayer
hole punch

Pencils and Crayons

Pencils and crayons are not only easy to handle but also give you many colors with which to work. Most young children learn to use them first before they begin to use paints.

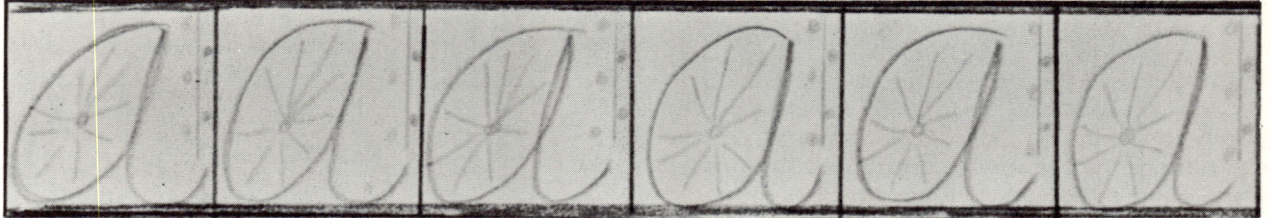

Pencils—plain and colored

The outline of the sailing boat shown in the picture below was drawn with an ordinary school pencil. The 10-year-old boy who drew it then used colored pencils to give light blue, green, gold, and brown effects. Colored pencils can also be use to make border designs for notebooks or a school bulletin board like the one shown above. To make a similar border design, just divide a piece of paper into equal sections and draw a capital letter and other decorations in each.

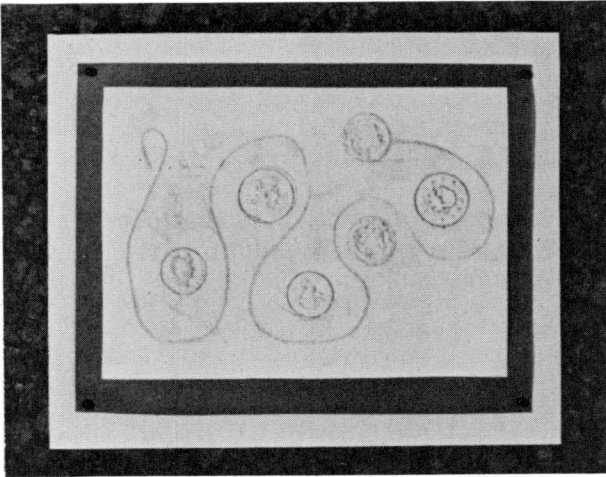

Making crayon rubbings

If you have ever put a piece of paper over a penny and scribbled a crayon over the paper until a picture of the coin appeared, you have made a **rubbing.** You can also make rubbings by using strings, odd shapes of paper, or leaves. Rub with the sides of peeled crayons.

Etching with crayons

Using the crayon point, cover the paper with a heavy coat of color—one color or many. Gently polish this with a paper towel. Now put on a heavy coat of **black crayon** and polish again. Using a **nail,** paper clip, or pin, scratch a design through the black coating down to the color.

OTHER WAYS TO USE CRAYONS

Designs on folded paper. Fold a sheet of drawing paper in half. With a wax crayon write your name in big letters above and on the crease. Refold the paper so that the writing is on the inside and press it with a warm iron. The colored wax in the crayon will print on the other half of the paper, making a design.

Crayon shavings. When you sharpen your crayons for drawing fine lines, save the shavings to make abstract pictures. Sprinkle them on colored construction paper, cover the paper with newsprint, and press it with a warm iron. The heat melts the crayon chips and makes interesting designs.

Crayon painting. Older children can make pictures by carefully softening the ends of wax crayons in the flame of a candle and painting with them on fairly heavy paper. The colors are very bright, and your picture will look like a thick oil painting.

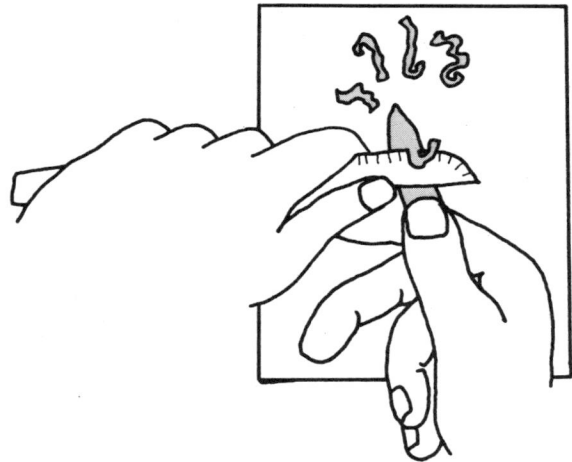

Paints, Chalk, and Felt Pens

One way that chalk, paint, and felt pens are different from pencils is that they cannot be erased from the paper. Carefully clean your paint brushes immediately after using them. Also, tightly close the lids on jars and put the caps on felt pens so they won't dry out.

Making a straw painting

Fun for everyone, these paintings are made by using a soda straw to blow pools of paint across the paper. First, place a blob or two of **poster paint** or **liquid acrylic** on a piece of **construction paper**. Then hold the **straw** close to the paint, and gently blow until the paint forms the design.

Using poster paint

Boys and girls will have fun making Christmas cards using **construction paper**, big **brushes**, and **poster paints**. This liquid paint can be purchased in jars or it can be made by mixing water with **powdered paint** (tempera); use a separate container for each color.

Nancy

Wet chalk painting

One way to make a wet chalk painting is to dip the **colored chalk** into water and draw on the **paper.** Another way is to put the drawing paper on newspapers, dampen it with a wet sponge, and then draw. This was the method that a first-grader used to make the picture of the bull-fighter shown above.

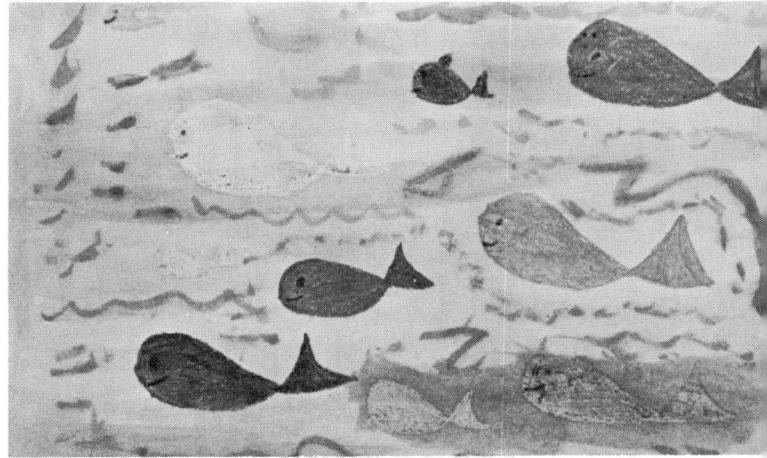

Water color wash

Draw a colorful design with **wax crayons.** Using an old **muffin tin** add drops of water to bright **acrylic paint** or poster paint until it is a watery color. This effect is called a wash. Brush the wash over the drawing. The background will be colored by the wash, but the crayon colors will stay the same.

HOW TO MAKE POSTERS

Here are the general rules for making good and easy-to-read posters:

1. Plan your design to fit the whole sheet of poster paper. Do not crowd it onto just one side of the paper. Try to balance the looks of it.

2. The most important picture you have to show or word you have to say should be the biggest and brightest on the poster. Use strong colors because pale colors are hard to see.

3. Make the printing clear and easy to read. It can be fancy if you are good at lettering or have stencils, but it must be readable.

4. Plan the lettering to be a part of the whole design. Fit it in with the pictures you use so that everything looks well together.

5. Choose pictures that have something to do with what the poster is about. They can be drawn directly on the poster paper, cut from magazines, or be one of your own drawings mounted and glued to the poster.

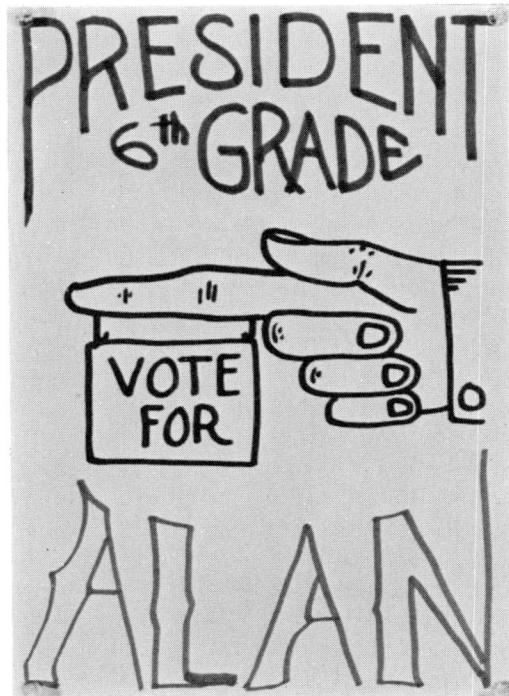

PRESIDENT 6th GRADE

VOTE FOR

ALAN

The fun of finger painting

Finger painting is fun because you do not need a lot of brushes or pencils. Just put your fingers into puddles of paint on the paper and spread it around until you make a pleasing picture.

How to make the paint. There are finger paint sets which you can buy, but if you want to use a lot of paint for many pictures, here is an easy way to make it:

Pour a cup of **liquid starch** into a **glass jar** or a **plastic container** that has a lid. Use a separate container for each color. Mix in **powered poster paint** (about a teaspoonful) a little at a time until it is the color you want to use.

How to finger paint. You will need **paper** with a glazed, hard surface—old magazine covers are very good. You can also use **butcher paper** or **drawing paper** covered with a heavy coat of **crayon**.

Place the paper on a table covered with newspapers. Using your hands, put the paint into the center of the paper and spread it over the whole sheet. Then, use your knuckles to make waves, your fist for swirls, your fingernails for lines, and the side of your hand for zig-zags.

If the paint begins to dry and becomes sticky before you have finished, mix in drops of water squeezed from a damp sponge, or keep a little bottle of water handy and add drops as they are needed.

Place your finished picture on another stack of newspapers to dry. If the dry picture curls at the edges, press the back of it with a warm iron.

Finger paint pictures can also be used as notebook covers or as wrapping for gifts.

Dip and dye

The entire family can enjoy making Japanese gift paper or wall hangings like the one shown at right. The paper, which is folded and then dipped into paint, has a soft, blurred look. It not only makes beautiful wrapping paper but is good for covering books and boxes.

What to use. The only unusual material you need is **rice paper**. If you cannot find this at an art store, any tough, absorbent paper—even paper towels—will do. You will also need **paint** (tubes of water color or acrylic), a **muffin tin** in which to mix the paint, **water,** and **paper towels.**

How to fold the paper. Fold the paper into a fan (as shown in the picture on the left below). Then fold the fan back and forth into triangles. On large sheets of paper the triangles will be farther apart than on small sheets. Fold plenty of paper before dipping, especially if several people are working.

How to dip-dye. Mix the paint and water, using a separate muffin cup for each color. Use plenty of paint if you want a deep color. As shown below in the right hand picture, dip each corner of the folded paper into the paint, letting it creep up into the paper. With your fingers and thumb, squeeze any extra paint out of the corners. **Carefully** unfold the wet paper and put it on paper towels to dry.

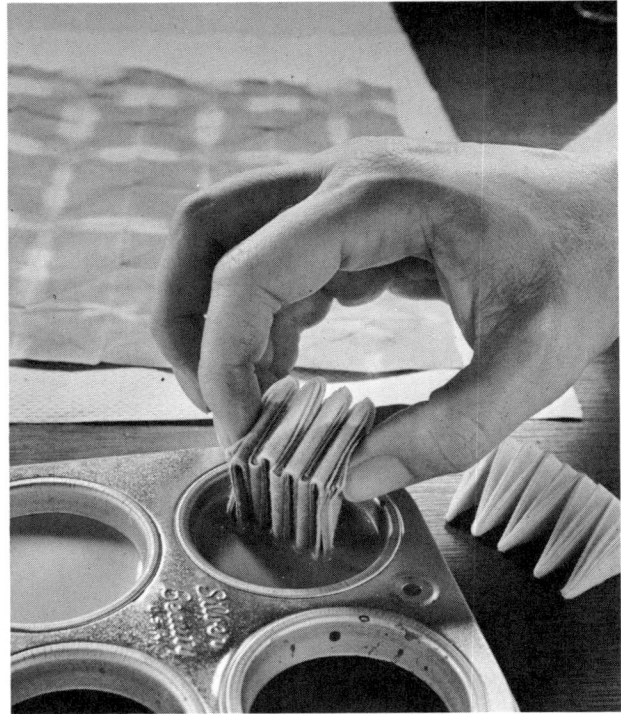

How to Make Prints on Paper

By using one of the printing methods shown below and on the next two pages, you can use the same design over and over to make greeting cards and gift wrapping. Cover the table where you are working with newspapers because you must press down hard when printing to make a clear print.

Printing with sponges

On a dry **plastic sponge** (which costs about 20 cents at a grocery store) draw or trace your design. Cut cleanly along the lines. A **craft knife** is a good cutting tool because it has a handle, but a razor blade may also be used—with care. Place **poster paint** in a dish, brush the paint onto the flat part of the sponge, and stamp it on your **paper**.

Printing with erasers

Draw your design on a **gum eraser** (which costs about 10 cents at a dime store). Use a **craft knife** to cut away the part around the design so the pattern is raised. On a piece of heavy **plastic** or **glass**, squeeze out **block printing ink**. Spread it thinly with a **brayer** (rubber roller), press the eraser in the ink, and then stamp it on the **paper**. When finished, clean tools with **turpentine**.

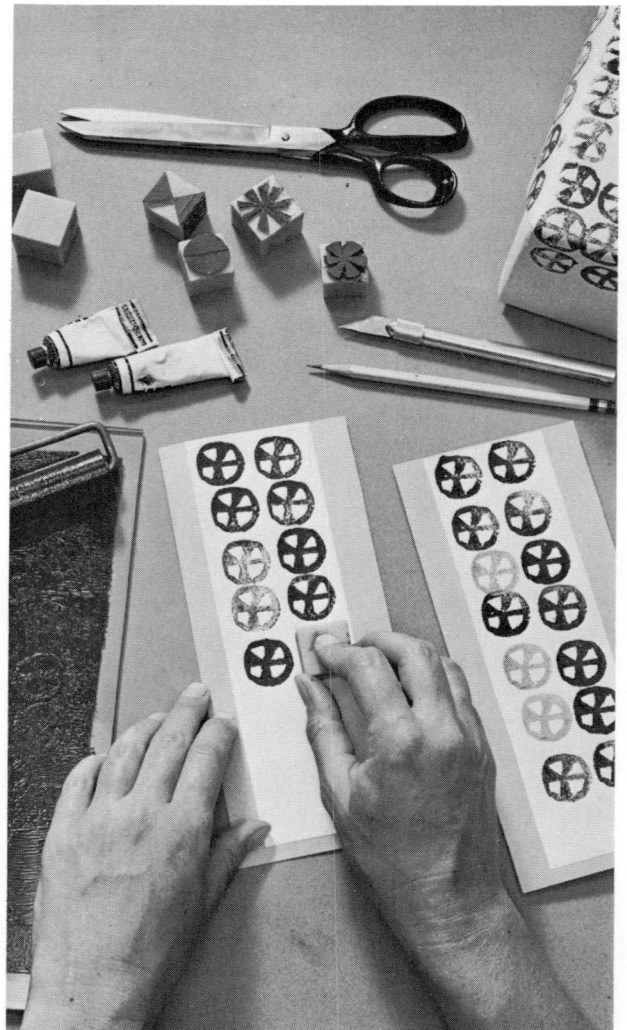

Making monoprints

Monoprint means **one** print. The picture is drawn with a stick on a piece of freshly painted glass or hard plastic. When a piece of paper is pressed against the glass or plastic, the design is printed. If you want to make more than one print, the glass must be repainted.

What you need. A piece of **glass** or **plastic** is used. The paint can be made from **canned evaporated milk** and powdered or liquid **poster paint.** This mixture can be cleaned off with water. A **brayer** is needed for rolling on the paint. Patterns are drawn with fingers or **sticks.** Use **construction paper** or **drawing paper** to print your design.

How to do it. Mix a half cup of canned milk with powdered or liquid poster paint using a separate jar for each color. With the brayer, spread a thin but even coat of paint over the piece of glass or plastic. (If the paint begins to get sticky, add a drop or two of water.) Now scratch a design using your finger or a stick. In the monoprint shown at right , a 7-year-old boy made lines with an old pencil. When your picture is finished, place a piece of paper over it, press evenly on the back, and lift off the monoprint.

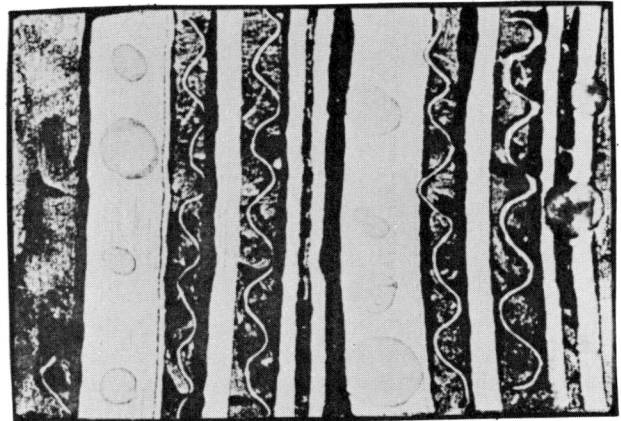

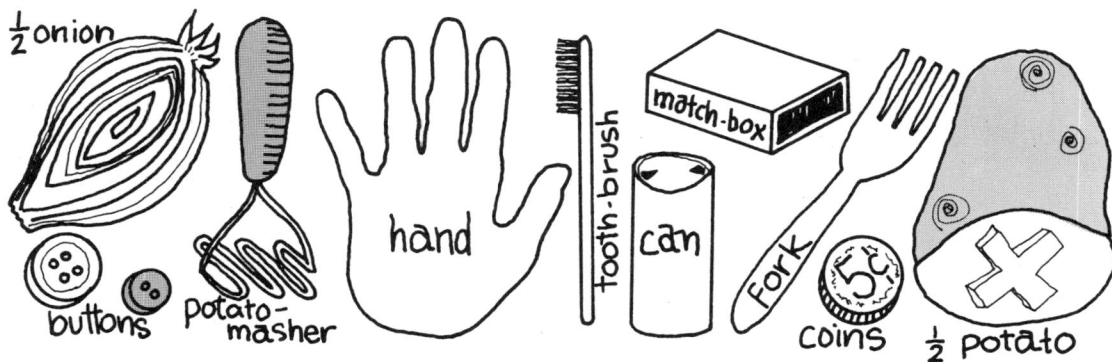

Printing with odds and ends

Interesting and easy prints can be made with **odds and ends** your mother has around the house. You will be surprised with the patterns you can make by pressing the bottom of a spice can or a bottle on an **ink pad** and then stamping your **paper.** Other things such as a matchbox, buttons, a fork, half an onion, or even your own hand, will also make unusual designs.

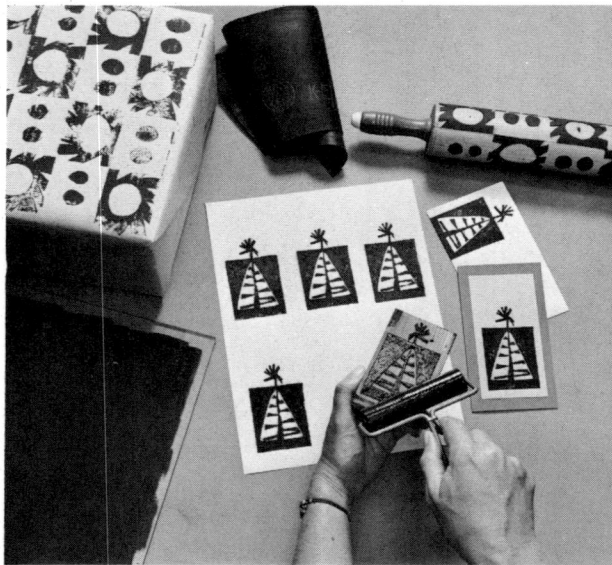

Printing with a rubber inner tube

Scraps from an **old rubber inner tube** (service stations usually have them) can be cut into various designs with **scissors**. Mount the design on a **wooden block, old rolling pin,** or thick **wooden dowel** using **white glue.** With a **brayer** (rubber roller), spread **block printing ink** on a piece of **plastic** or **glass.** When the roller has an even coating of ink on it, roll it over the rubber design on the block. Press firmly or roll the inked side of the design on your paper.

Making block prints

Older boys and girls enjoy block printing because there is no limit to the number of copies or the combination of colors. In the linoleum block print shown below on the right, the design shows the cut half of an orange.

What you need. You will need a few special tools. At a craft store buy a **linoleum block,** a **brayer** (also called an ink roller), 2 or 3 V-shaped **gouges** in different sizes, and washable **printing ink.** You will also need an old **cooky sheet** or a piece of glass, and construction or drawing **paper.**

How to block print. First draw a design and then trace it onto the linoleum block. Gouge along the lines, using a big gouge for wide lines and a small one for narrow lines. Handle the tools very **carefully** because they are sharp! After squeezing the ink onto the cooky sheet, roll the brayer in the ink. Then roll the brayer over the block, covering it evenly with ink. Press the paper against the block and rub firmly so that a good print will be made.

Things to Make with Paper

The first part of this chapter has shown how to make drawings and prints on paper. You can also do different things **with** paper: the texture can be changed by making the flat surface rough with holes or weaving, and different shapes can be made by cutting, tearing, folding, or pasting many layers together.

Notebooks and folders

Booklets can be made to hold photographs, drawings, and other collections. Leaves or flowers can be pressed and displayed beautifully in a folder like the one shown above. To make one like it, accordian pleat a long strip of fairly **heavy paper** the size you want. Staple a piece of **yarn** to the back cover for a tie.

To make another type of notebook, fold several sheets of **construction paper** in half. Fit the sheets together and at the center fold, make holes through all the sheets using a **paper punch** or nail. Then, with a large **needle**, put a piece of heavy yarn through each hole, pull it tight, and tie a knot on the outside of the folder. Finish by decorating.

HOW TO FRAME PICTURES

The easiest way to make a frame for a favorite picture or drawing is to paste it carefully in the center of a slightly larger sheet of **construction paper.** The color of the paper should look well with the picture. Here are other ideas:

Shadow box frame. Place your picture in the middle of a larger sheet of construction paper. Then, with a pencil, lightly trace around the shape of the picture. Remove the picture and, with a ruler and a pencil, lightly draw a line from each corner of the picture to each corner of the construction paper. Fold the paper toward you on the lines around the picture. Then, pinch together and fold the lines from the corners inward to the other folded lines. Glue the picture in place and it will have a shadow box frame.

Paper frame or mat. Center the picture on a piece of construction or lightweight **poster paper** that is about 2 inches wider than the picture. Lightly trace around the picture and remove it from the paper. Then cut out a window that is about a quarter inch smaller than the traced outline of the picture. Place the picture behind the frame so that it can be seen through the window and glue it in place. This is called matting a picture.

Board frame. Find a lightweight **board** that is larger than your picture. Cover it with a piece of **cloth** or felt, pulling the edges of the material to the back and **stapling** or **gluing** them in place. Trim the edges of the picture and center it on the cloth-covered board, gluing it down with rubber cement or white glue.

Torn paper pictures

Beautiful pictures can be made by using torn or cut pieces of colored paper. You can also use pieces of paper to decorate cards or notebook covers. Use **construction paper** or any soft paper that tears easily. Paste the torn designs onto another piece of paper with **rubber cement** or **white glue**.

Tissue paper pictures

You have never seen real flowers as big and bright as the ones below! They are really scraps of **tissue paper** overlapped and glued down with **rubber cement**. The tissue, which is brilliantly colored and inexpensive, can also be crinkled, twisted, and folded. The angel picture shown at right was brushed with a coat of **polymer medium** to give it a shiny appearance.

Tissue paper flowers

A pretty bouquet of paper flowers is fun to make and is a nice gift for your mother. Choose a vase or jelly glass that goes well with the flower colors. The vase in the picture at right is blue and the flowers are bright blue, light blue, and grassy green.

What to use. Tissue paper in three shades of the same color, or several different colors. **Straight pins** to hold the petals together. **Florist tape** to wrap the pin and stems. This tape is green and sticky, and you can buy it at the dime store. **Thin wire**, cut in 8-inch lengths, for the stems.

How to do it. Trace the petal patterns from the drawing below using the darkest shade of paper when tracing the outside line and lighter paper for the inside lines. Cut out the patterns and stack them one on top of the other putting the largest petal on the bottom. Stick a pin in the center dot, down through all three layers. Push the petals up over the head of the pin. Then hold the pin tightly against a piece of wire and wrap the florist tape snugly around the pin and the wire as well as the bottom of the petals.

For different looking flowers, cut curvy petals or fringes as the drawing shows.

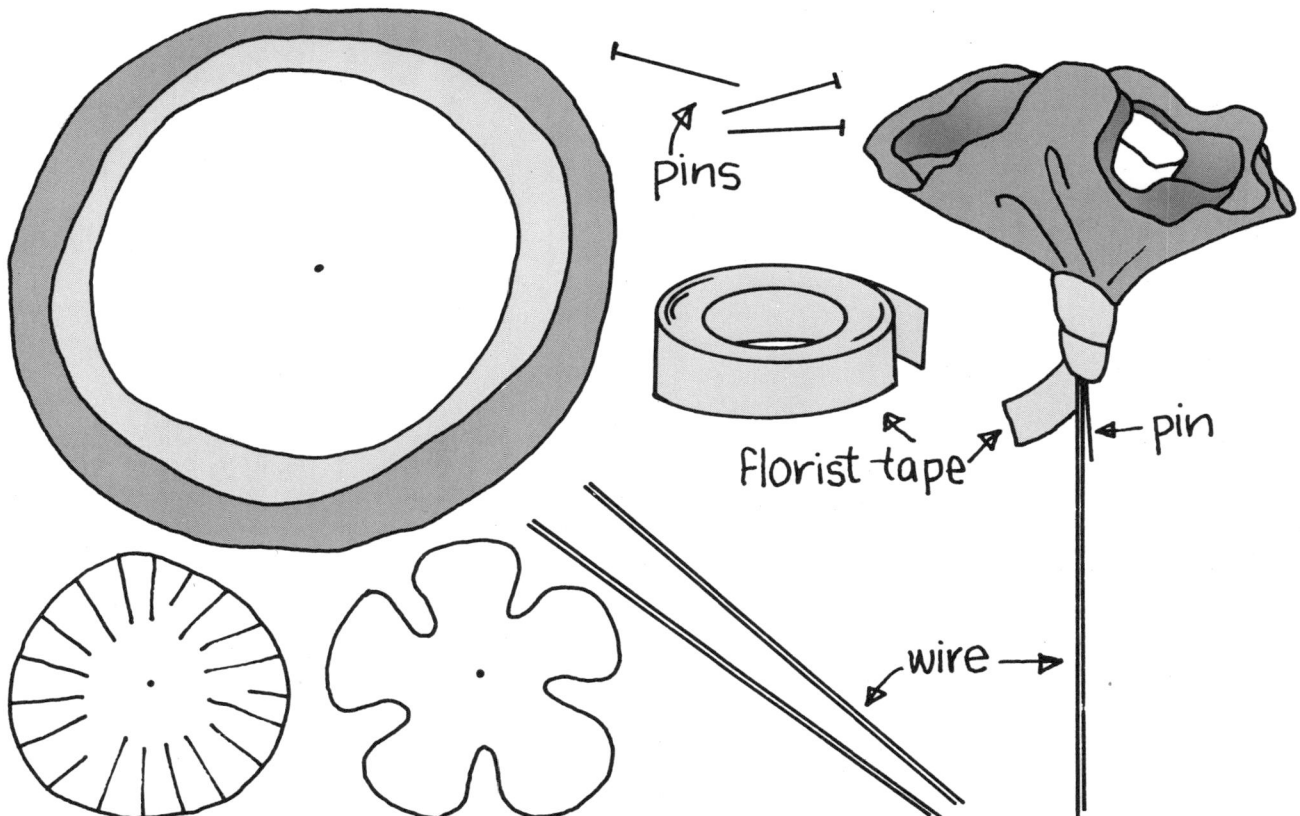

pins

florist tape

pin

wire →

Decorated paper pinwheels

Pinwheels are happy things. They are bright and whirl gaily in a breeze or when you blow on them. Another nice thing is that they are so easy to make. Even boys and girls who haven't started to school yet can make them with a little help.

What you need. Stiff poster paper is best to use because it doesn't tear easily, but you can also use heavy construction paper. Decorate your pinwheel with **crayon, poster paint,** or **felt pen** designs. You will need **scissors,** a **straight pin, sticky tape,** a small **cardboard** circle about a half inch wide, and a **stick** for a handle.

How to do it. Trace the pattern below, cut this square from a piece of stiff paper. Be sure to mark the letters and dots in the middle and the four corners. Also, draw the lines that go **almost** to the middle, and then cut along these lines with your scissors. Now bend (don't fold) the points marked A, B, C, and D to the middle dot and tape them together. Push a straight pin through the center of the small cardboard circle marked E, then through the taped points, and into a stick, an eraser of an unsharpened pencil, or a drinking straw. Then blow and watch it spin.

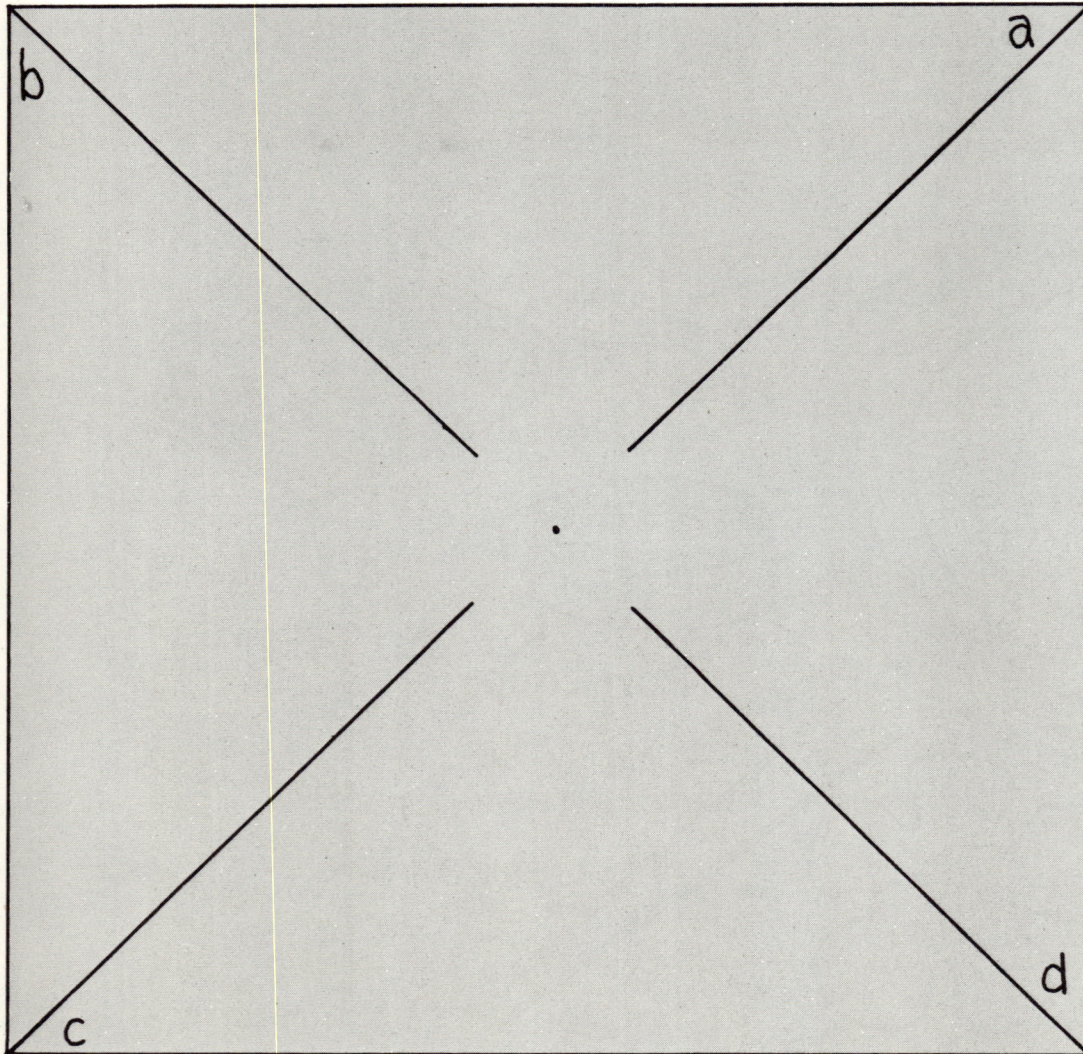

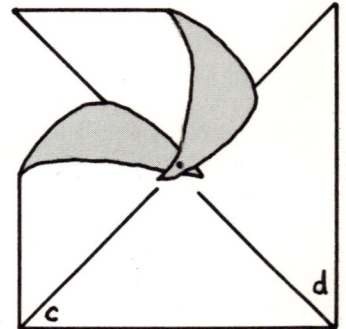

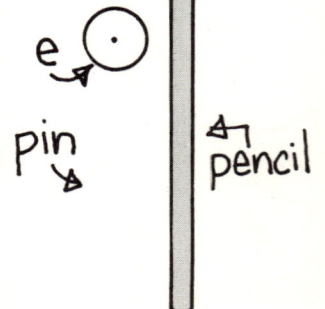

Punches, cuts, and fringes

A piece of paper doesn't always have to be flat. The three pictures below show just a few ways to change the paper's surface—its face. Perhaps you can think up some other ways. In the picture on the left, the design was made by punching big and little holes using **pencils** and toothpicks. In the middle picture, an ordinary rectangle was cut apart with curving lines and then pasted onto **dark paper**. In the picture on the right, wavy lines were cut across the paper and folded open like little, long doors. Then tiny slits or fringes were cut on the flaps.

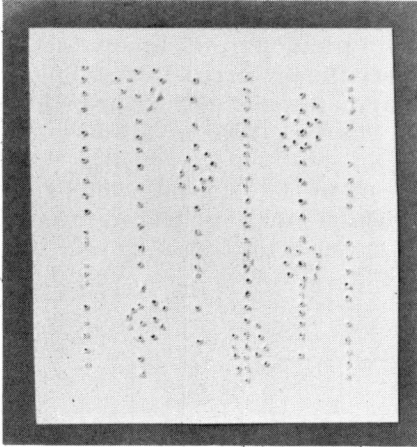

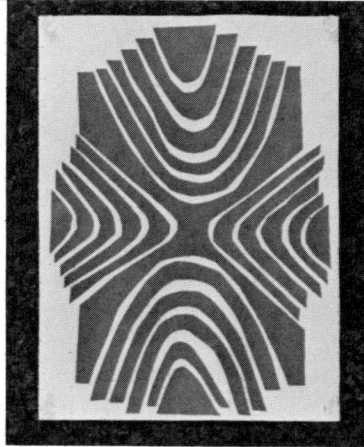

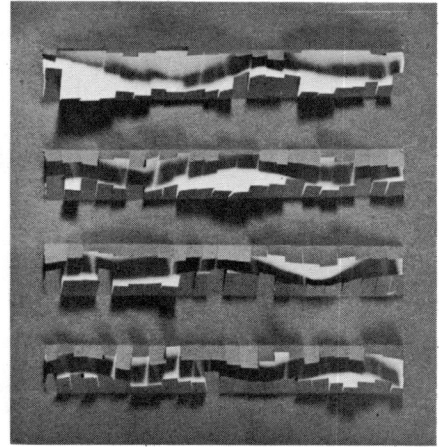

Weaving with paper

Simple mats can be made by weaving single strips of **colored paper** through another piece of paper that has been already cut along drawn lines (see the picture below on the left). Using a heavy piece of **construction paper**, draw the lines almost to the edges. Carefully cut along these lines. Then cut several strips from another piece of paper. Weaving the first strip **under** one cut and **over** the next, work across the mat. Then weave the second strip **over** one and **under** the next. Continue weaving until the mat is filled. The picture on the right below is an example of weaving a design by making wavy cuts and strips.

Three paper chains

Chains are lively decorations for a party or for Christmas, but most of all, they are fun to make.

The picture at left shows three different types of chains. The chain on the right is the easiest to make. First cut a piece of **construction paper** into strips. Take the first strip and join the two ends together with **sticky tape** or glue. Take a second strip, run it through the first loop and join its ends together. In the same way, add as many loops as you want to the chain.

The middle chain is made from paper which is folded in two. Trace the pattern below and place it on the folded paper. Cut as many of these links as you need and connect them as the drawing shows.

The chain links on the left are cut from double folded paper on which you have traced the pattern shown below. Open up the links and join them as shown in the drawing.

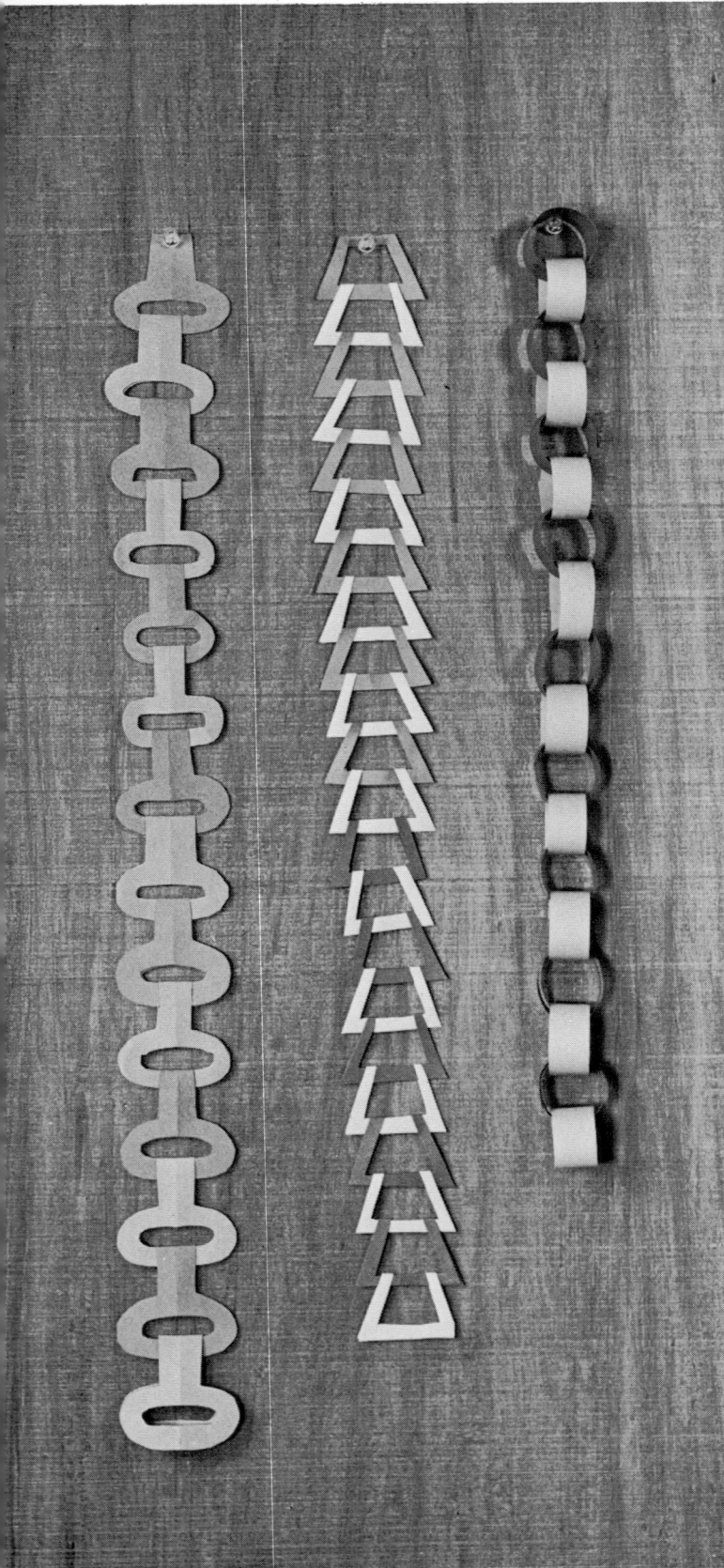

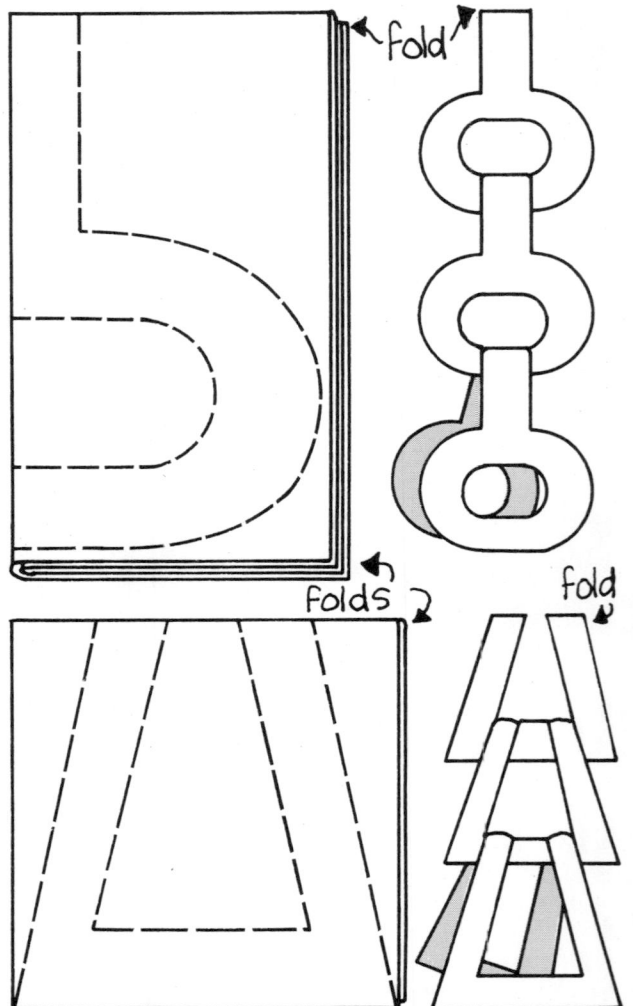

Curled paper snails

This herd of paper snails would look right at home next to a flower arrangement or one of your mother's houseplants. They are made from curled strips of **construction paper.** Tiny curled strips are glued on for antennae.

Strips of paper can easily be curled if you pull them firmly through your fingers or across a pair of scissors.

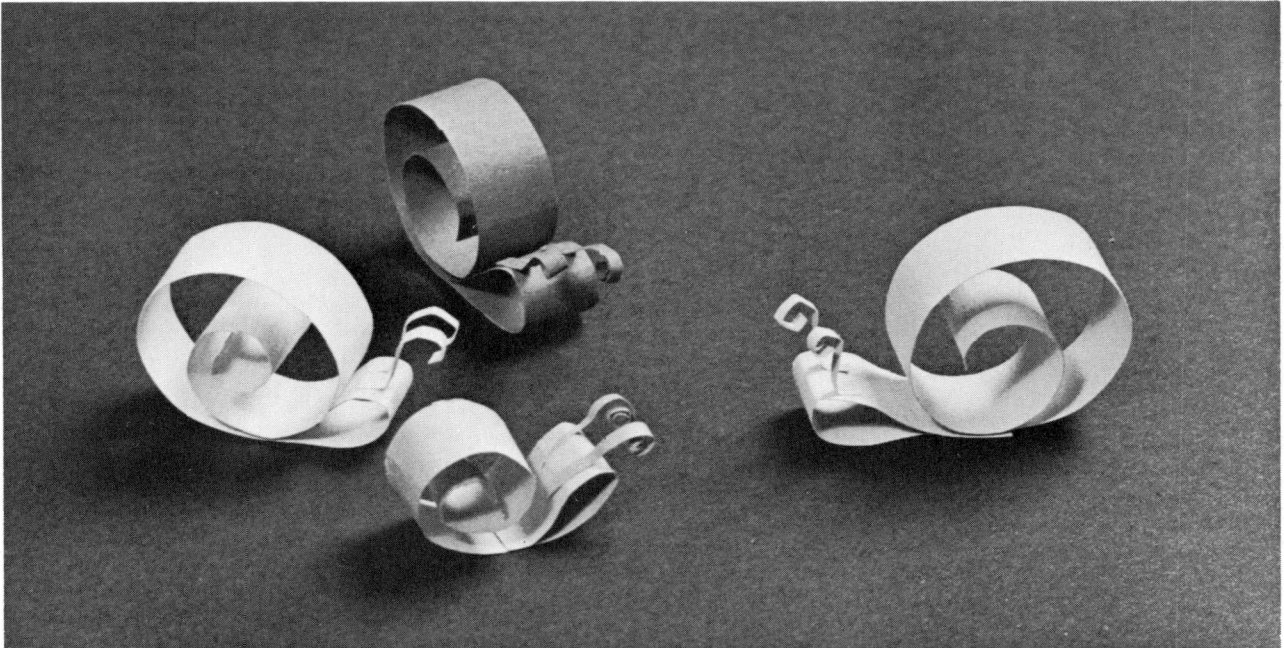

A cylinder city

An eight-year-old girl constructed these paper tubes and thought they looked like a group of city buildings. She cut **drawing paper** into several different lengths and widths and pulled the pieces of paper firmly over a table edge to make them curl. Then she joined the edges together with **glue** (you can also use your stapler or clear, sticky tape) to make the cylinder shapes.

A cylinder figure

This figure, with a bunch of tiny flowers in the top, is another example of what you can do with an ordinary paper cylinder. Add a halo and a set of wings as shown in the picture below, and you have an angel for a Christmas scene.

What to use. Large sheets of heavy **drawing paper** are best to use but construction paper will work equally as well if you are making small figures. You will need a **craft knife** for cutting and **glue** for joining the cylinder ends.

How to do it. Follow the drawing shown below and **lightly** draw the face, eyes, nose, hand, and sleeveline in the center of your paper. Where the line is dotted, **score** the paper. Scoring means to lightly cut along the line with your knife, but not all the way through. Then cut along the other lines. Glue the ends of the paper together to make a cylinder. Then gently fold and push along the scored face line to bend it inward. Add a bunch of flowers or two wings and a halo.

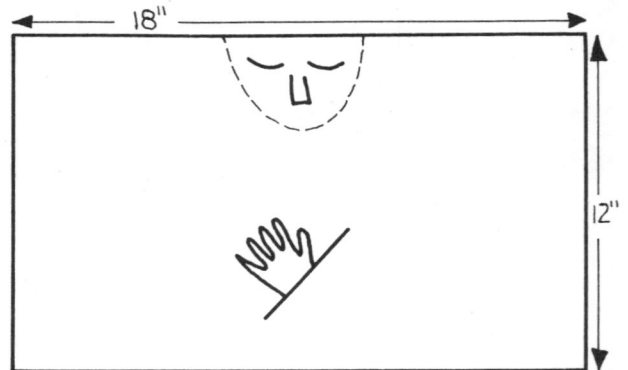

Two kinds of greeting cards

Cards which are fancy or pop up when opened will surprise friends on their birthdays.

How to make pop-ups. When this card is opened, a bear pops up. To make the bear card shown at right, fold a piece of paper in half and draw the lines of the bear over the center fold. Cut along the lines, but be sure not to cut the paws loose as that is how the bear hangs on to the paper.

How to use puffy tissue. The fancy flowers and sheep decorating the birthday cards shown below are made with tiny squares of colored **tissue paper** which are glued to a piece of white **drawing paper**. First fold the paper and then plan where you want the design. Cut the tissue into a lot of little half-inch squares. Place the eraser end of a **pencil** in the middle of each square and fold it up around the pencil. Then dip the tissue covered end of the pencil into **white glue** and press the square into place on the card. Do this over and over until you have finished the design.

Paper ornaments for Christmas

Here are two gay ornaments for decorating a Christmas tree. Both are quite easy to make and will fold flat so you can send them as cards or put them away for the next Christmas.

Three-tiered ornament. To make this Chirstmas ornament, cut six squares of **construction or drawing paper,** following the drawing below. Fold each square along the diagonal dotted lines. Then, turn the square over and fold it in half in both directions, but this time make a crease only halfway from the center to the edge. Take two squares and glue the points of one to the points of the other. Be sure to keep the diagonal folds to the inside. When you have made the three tiers, glue them together at the centers. Place a **string hanger** on top and add a paper tail.

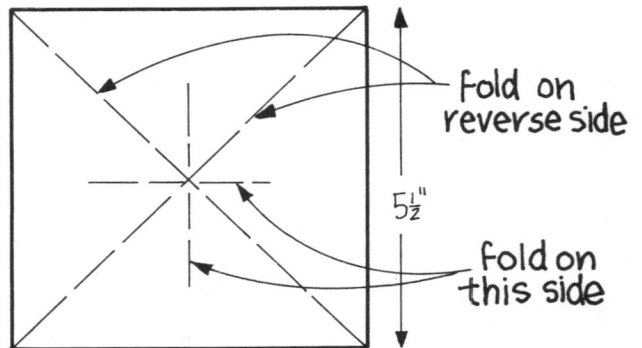

fold on reverse side

$5\frac{1}{2}''$

fold on this side

Partridge in a pear tree. A bright paper partridge swings gently among the leaves of a pear tree mobile. Following the drawing below, make two **construction paper** trees for each ornament. Glue points of leaves together. Then cut out a paper bird and hang it by a **thread** taped to the inside top of the tree. Tape a thread hanger to the top of the tree. At the bottom, hang a cut out pear and leaf on a short thread.

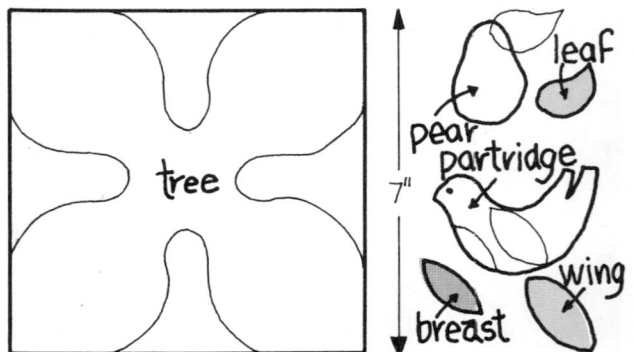

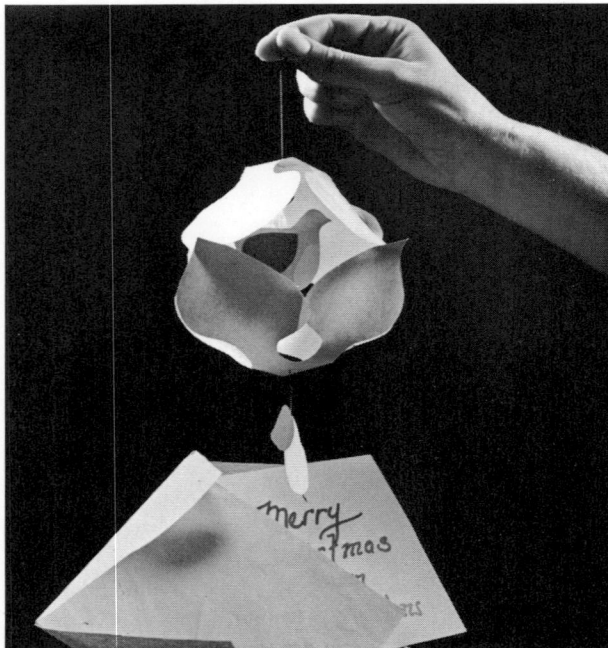

tree

7"

leaf

pear partridge

breast

wing

Two decorations from the same pattern

The two decorations shown on this page do not look alike, but they are made from the same pattern. Both are pleated like fans and then designs are cut out. You can use almost any kind of lightweight paper. It can also be any size, but the general shape should be a little less than half as wide as it is long.

Wall hanging. For the wall hanging use two sheets of **paper,** one a little smaller than the other. Accordion-fold papers together into 8 equal pleats. Separate papers and refold each on the pleat lines. Cut round corners on the pleat ends. On the folded edges cut out two half circles. Unfold each fan and place the smaller one over the larger. Use **staples** to hold them together. Fold each end of your hanging over a small **stick** or dowel, staple the folded parts together, and put it up on a wall.

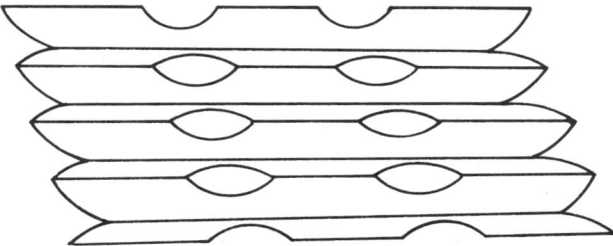

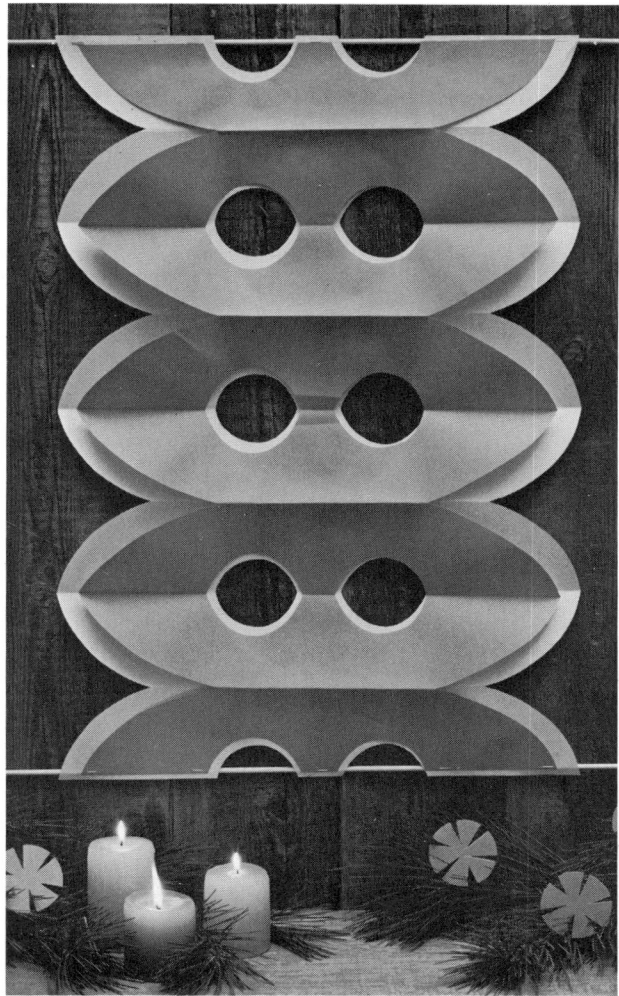

Medallion. Fold a sheet of **paper** into 8 equal parts. Follow the drawing shown above used for making the wall hanging, round the pleat corners and cut half circles on the folded edges. Then take a **needle** and **thread** and stitch through the center of the folds. Following the drawing below, pull the center folds together and tie the thread. Make the medallion circle by bringing the top and bottom edges together and taping underneath.

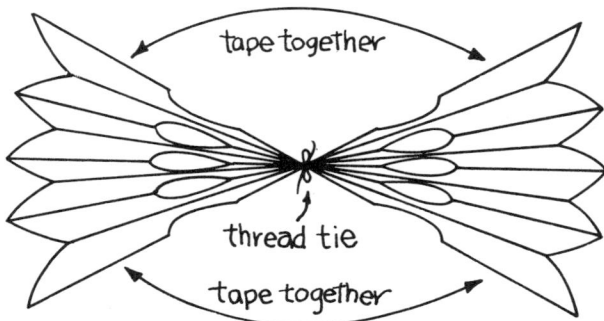

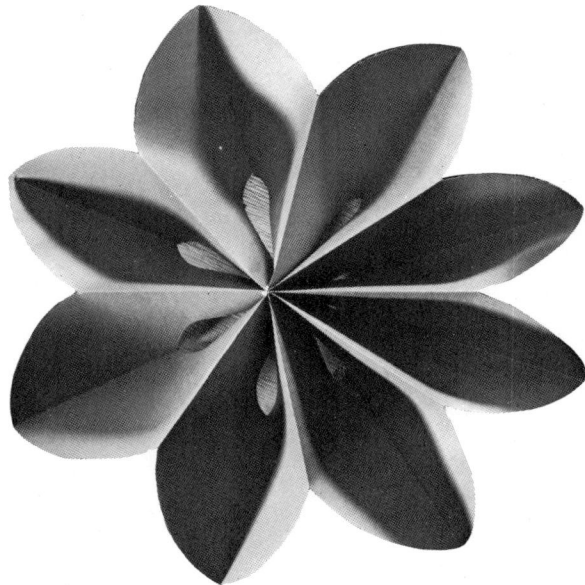

Papier Mache Projects

You can make colorful gifts or decorations for your room using a very old craft material called **papier mache** (these words are French and mean chewed paper). Papier mache isn't exactly chewed but the paper is torn, cut, or wadded up, and then coated with some kind of paste. The projects below and on the next three pages show several different ways of making papier mache. You can also buy instant papier mache powder at a craft store. Just add water to get a pulp something like clay, which can be used for small projects.

Pins to wear

Fifth graders made these pins using lightweight **cardboard**, narrow strips of torn **newspaper**, and a **white glue-water** mixture. Cut the shapes from the cardboard and cover them with quarter-inch strips of newspaper dipped into the glue-water (a half cup of white glue mixed with a quarter cup of water). Continue adding strips until the shape has been covered 3 or 4 times. Put the pins in a 200° oven until dry. Paint with **acrylic paints** and glue a **clasp** to the back.

Beads to string

You will need long, quarter-inch strips of **paper towels** to make these beads. One at a time, dip each strip into a pan of full-strength **liquid starch**. Squeeze off any extra starch and wrap the strip around a **metal knitting needle**. Use as many layers of strips as you want for each bead. Dry the beads (still on the needle) in a 200° oven, and paint with **acrylics**. Slip the dry beads off the needle and string them onto a piece of **yarn** or a leather thong.

A holder for pencils

This elephant holds pencils in the top of his head instead of his trunk.

What to use. The elephant's body is made from a frozen **orange juice can** covered with several layers of **newspaper**. Each layer is pasted down with **white glue**. When the ears and trunk are in place, the elephant is painted with **acrylic paint** and **buttons** are used for his eyes.

How to do it. Once you have finished covering the orange juice can, then make the elephant's ears. Cut four circles of newspaper for each ear and glue one on top of the other. Then cut a slit to the center of each ear as shown in the picture below on the left. Slightly overlap and glue the slit ends to form conelike ears. While the paper is still wet with glue, ruffle the ears a little and attach them to the body. Make a trunk by gluing together four long rectangles of paper. Crumple the trunk into a curve and attach it with glue or tape.

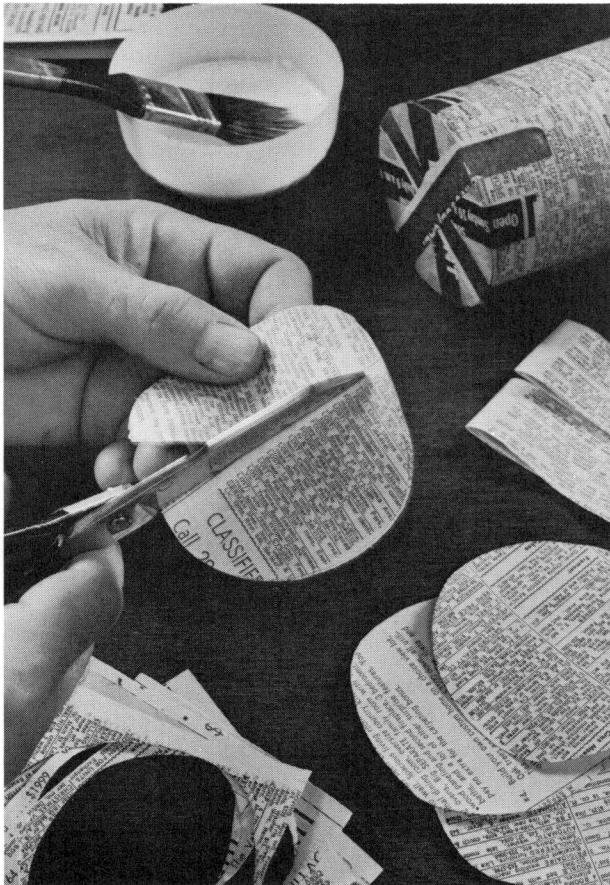

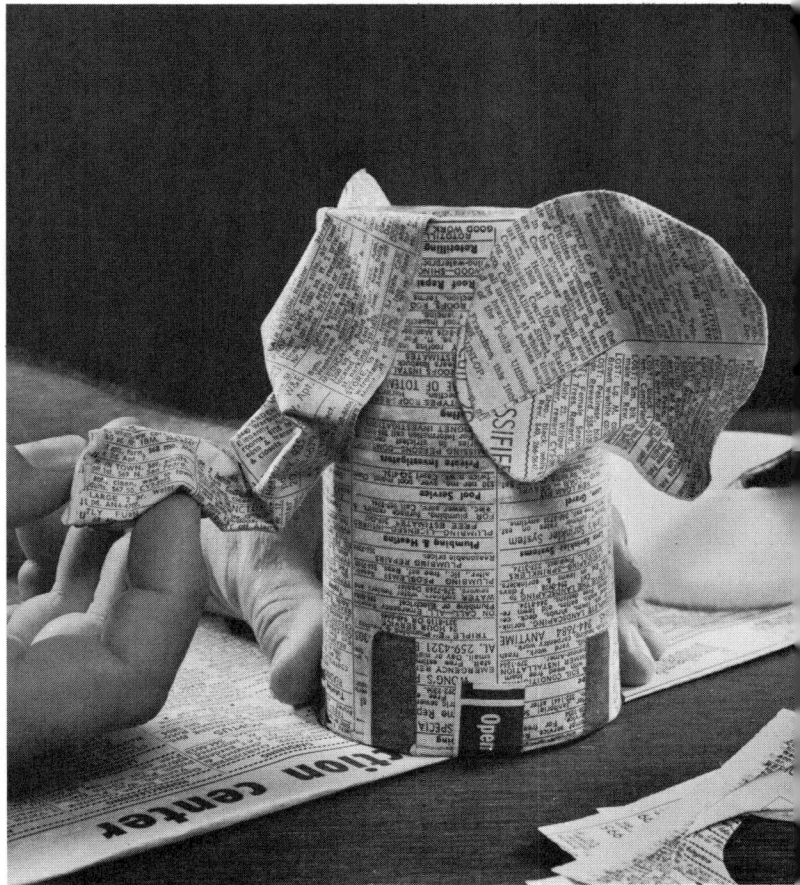

An owl bank

This owl-shaped bank will hold a lot of pennies and nickels because it was made with papier mache strips over a plump balloon.

What to use. You need a **balloon** for the body and strips of **newspaper** which are dipped in **wheat paste** or **liquid starch** to cover it. **Cardboard** is used for the feet and the base. Before the bank is painted a coat of **polymer medium** can be brushed on to make a hard surface for the **acrylic paint**.

What to do. First blow up the balloon. Then, as the picture below on the left shows, put on a layer of newspaper strips dipped in clear water (this will make the balloon easy to remove). Add two more layers of strips after dipping them into wheat paste or starch. The last row of papier mache should end in an even, neat line near the bottom of the balloon. Next, cut out paper cones for the ears and beak as shown in the middle picture. Glue them onto the body and cover them with three layers of strips. When the owl is partly dry, pop the balloon and remove it.

As the picture below on the right shows, cut the feet from heavy cardboard. For the base, cut a strip of cardboard and tape the ends together to form a circle. Be sure that the circle fits the body. Tape the base to the feet and build up the feet with dipped paper strips. Coat with **polymer medium**, if you wish. Use a knife to cut the money slot, and then paint the owl.

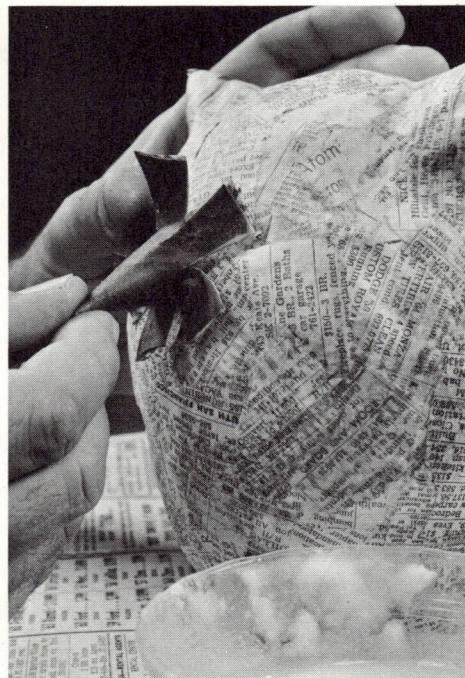

Papier mache zoo

Modeling clay and paper towels are used to make the papier mache animals parading across this page.

What you need. Any kind of modeling clay can be used but it is a good idea to buy **non-hardening clay.** It is gray in color and stays soft and workable. You also need white **paper towels** torn in strips, full-strength **liquid starch,** and melted **paraffin** to cover the clay form so that it can be removed later. The animals can be painted with brilliant **acrylic colors** and, if you wish, you can also give them a shiny coat of **polymer medium.** This is a liquid that is brushed on and can be purchased at any art store.

How to make each animal. Push, pinch, and squeeze the clay until it is soft. Use big pieces for the body and small wads for the feet, head, and tail.

(If you want to use the clay another time, ask your mother to melt some paraffin for you. Using an old brush, completely cover the body with paraffin. This will keep the papier mache from sticking.)

Now start covering the animal with paper towel strips dipped in liquid starch. Cover the whole form with three or four layers and let it dry for a day or two. **Do not put it in the oven,** because the clay will melt!

If you plan to use the clay again, slice the dry animal in two with a sharp knife. The clay will slip out easily. Fit the hollow animal together, cover the cut with papier mache, and let it dry a second time. Then paint the animal with acrylics and brush on a coat of polymer medium.

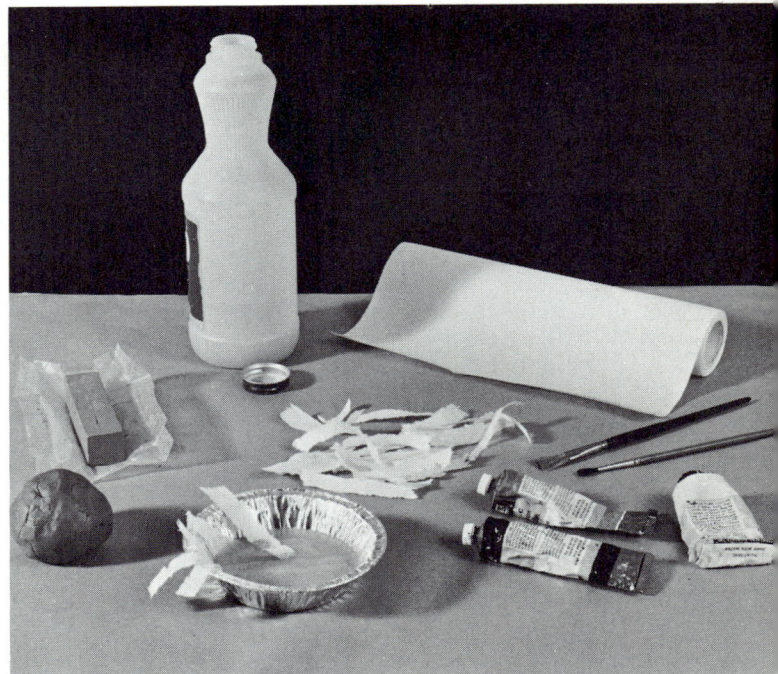

More Paper Projects

Here are just a few more ideas for working with paper. You will find hundreds of other ways, too, of turning a plain piece of paper into a project that will please you.

Make your own paper bags

It is very easy to make a supply of fancy paper bags for your lunches or to hold gifts. All you need is some **heavy paper**. You can use gift paper, or shelf paper which you have decorated with paint, or block or stamp prints. You also need something on which to form the bag—a block of **wood**, a brick, a milk carton, or a sturdy cereal or shoe box.

How to make the bags. Cut your paper big enough to wrap around the form you have chosen—a brick, box, or block of wood. Then follow the three steps shown in the pictures below: **1.** With your fingers, crease along the sides and bottom of the paper to make the folds. **2.** Glue the sides of the paper together to make a back seam and fold in the bottom (leave the top open). Glue the bottom well. **3.** Take the bag off the form and fold the creases firmly starting at the top and working toward the bottom. On the back seam side, fold the bottom of the bag upward.

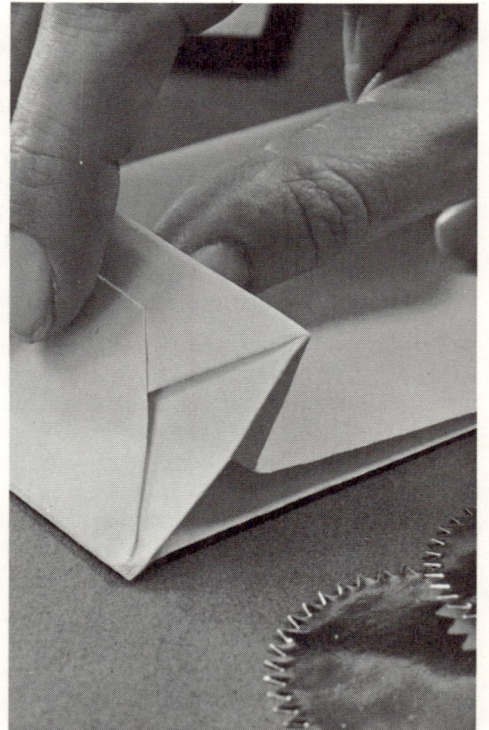

A snowman mobile

You can construct this wintertime mobile using **heavy paper** and **thread.** From white paper, cut out a circle about 7 inches across for the snowman's base. Also cut a 6-inch circle for the body, and a 5-inch circle for the head. Make black paper hands and hat, and a red scarf. Glue the hands to the body circle and then glue on the black eyes, nose, and mouth. Put an orange pipe in the snowman's mouth. Using a **needle,** punch holes in the top and bottom of each mobile part and attach them together with thread.

A ladybug table setting

A big, bright ladybug nearly covers this place mat. Smaller bugs decorate the paper cup and napkin ring. Use a sheet of light colored **construction paper** for the mat. Make two big circles the same size—one from orange paper and the other from brown paper. Cut a smaller circle from the brown paper for the head. To make the bug's wings, take the orange paper circle and cut small circles and a slit. Paste the brown circle under the wings. Glue the head and body to the mat and add narrow strips of brown paper for antennae. Smaller bugs are made the same way.

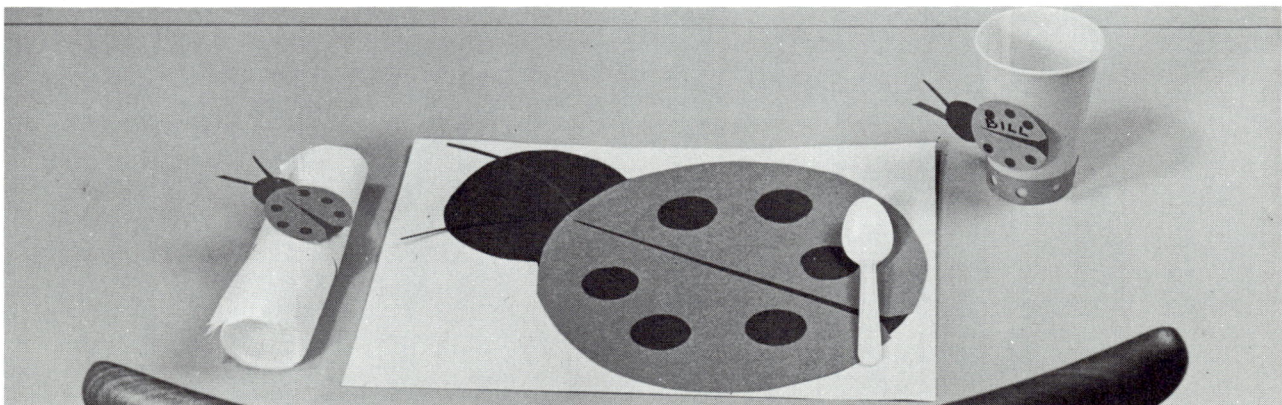

CLOTH CRAFTS

DECORATED TAGS & NOTE PAPER • BOOKENDS • BOOKMARKS
"PAPER" DOLL & DRESSES • CLOTH SCRAP PICTURE • EMBROIDERY STITCH CHART
STITCHERY PICTURES & WALL HANGINGS • PINCUSHIONS • EASY WEAVING
BATIK • SPRAY PAINT STENCILS • IRON-ON DESIGNS • FELT PEN & CRAYON DESIGNS

Tags and note paper

It takes only a few minutes to turn out a stack of gay gift tags like the ones shown below on the right. Glue 2-inch scraps of fringed **burlap** to the edges of small, folded pieces of **paper**. The paper can be plain or you can cover it with foil. Decorate the tags with cutouts from old greeting cards or with tiny **ornaments**. The note paper shown below on the left is simply plain **stationery** with **cut-out cloth** designs glued to the upper corner. You can decorate envelope flaps in the same way.

Boy-and-girl bookends

These two friendly bookends are really round **oatmeal boxes** covered with cloth. First, fill the boxes with sand, and tape on the tops. For the faces, measure not quite half way down from the top of each box and cover these parts with light **felt**. **White glue** will hold the felt and other parts in place. Eyes and noses are circles of felt. Use red and blue **cloth** for the boy's suit and flowered fabric for the girl's dress. Attach long strips of matching felt for the arms and legs and cut **cotton yarn** into 10-inch lengths for hair.

Four colorful bookmarks

Anyone who likes to read would enjoy receiving a bookmark. The ones shown below are especially colorful and easy to make from scraps of **felt**. The giraffe and flower bookmarks are about 10 inches long. The smaller cat and mouse bookmark is good for little books about 7 inches long.

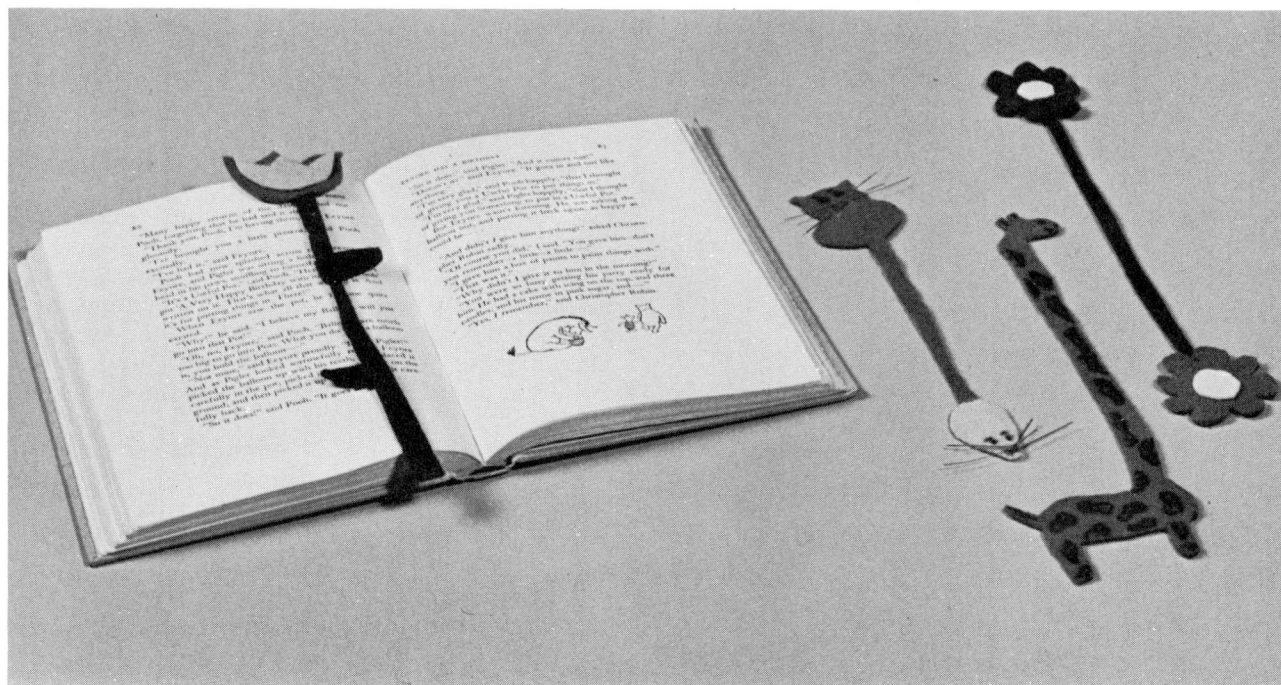

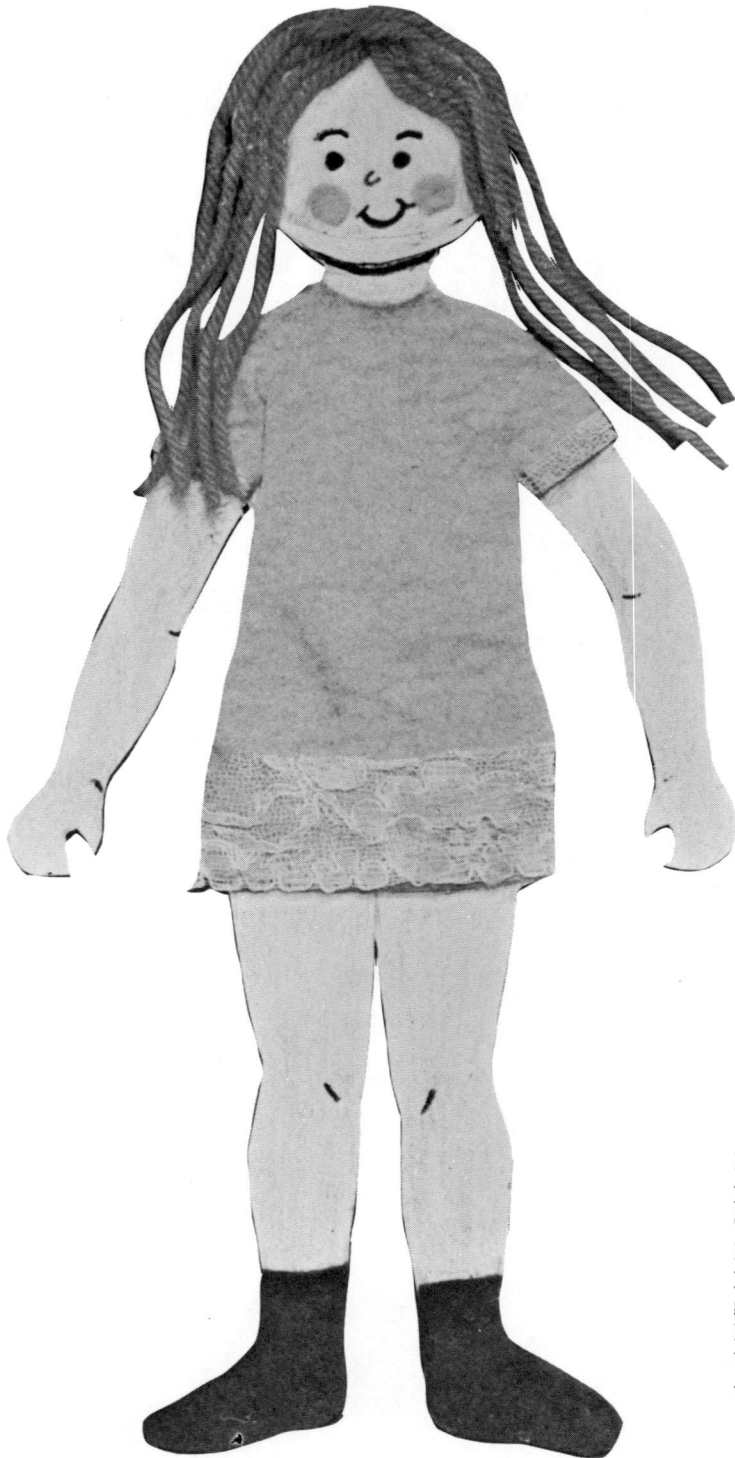

"Paper" doll with a cloth dress

Little girls will like this doll which is made from paper and wears a pink felt dress. Other cloth dresses cling to the pink dress when they are pressed into place. Trace the doll outline on this page and transfer it to **heavy paper.** Using **white glue,** attach **yarn** hair, a **felt** dress, and shoes. Draw on a smiling face with crayons. A shoe box, decorated inside like a bedroom, is a handy way to carry your doll to a friend's house.

A wardrobe for your paper doll

You can get some other ideas for using **cloth scraps** from the doll dresses shown below. Trace the dress pattern on the opposite page and transfer it to a piece of cloth. Cut out the dress and add trimmings of lace, buttons, or other scraps.

A cloth scrap picture

"Butterflies in a Hurry" is the name given this picture by the 8-year-old girl who made it. She used cloth scraps from dresses her mother had saved. First she cut out butterfly shapes, glued them in place on **poster paper**, and made antennae and bodies from one long piece of **black yarn**. Then she outlined each butterfly with a black **felt pen** and used black sticky-backed **tape** on the edges of the picture for a frame.

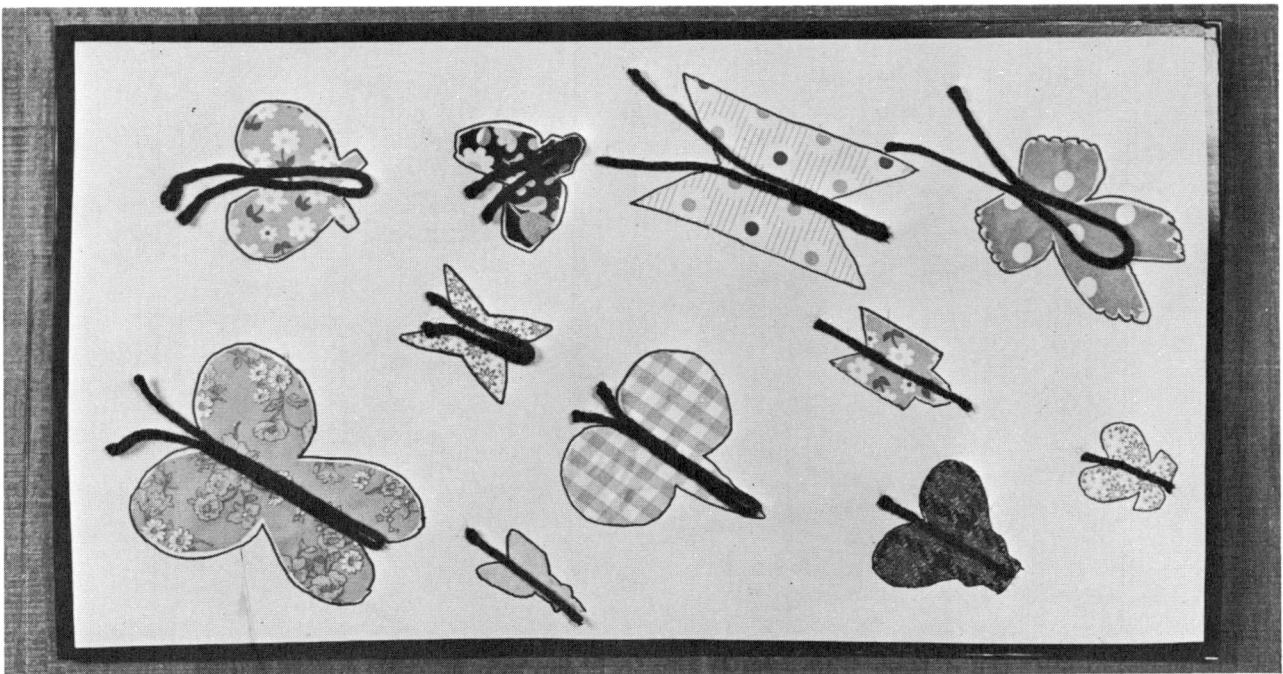

Stitchery and Other Designs on Cloth

The first projects in this chapter have shown how you can use cloth in much the same way you use paper—you can cut it out and glue it down for decorations, and you can also use it to wrap boxes and gifts. The following pages give instructions on how to make designs on cloth with stitchery (which is another name for embroidery and decorative sewing), weaving, stencil and batik painting, and crayon and felt pen drawings.

HOW TO MAKE EMBROIDERY STITCHES

Embroidery means sewing plain or fancy stitches in a design to make a picture. For each project on this and the following three pages, the instructions tell you the kind of stitch to use. The drawings below show you how to make each of these stitches.

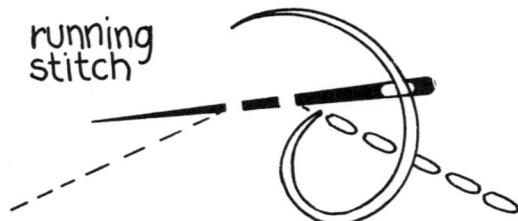

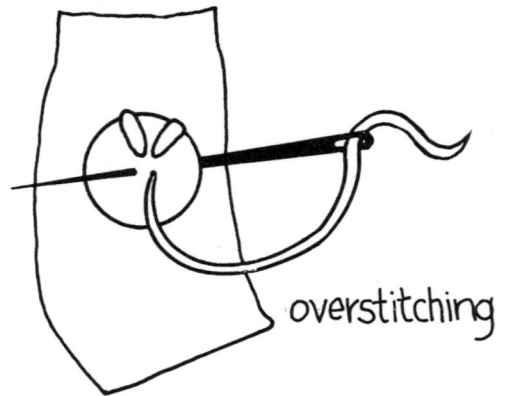

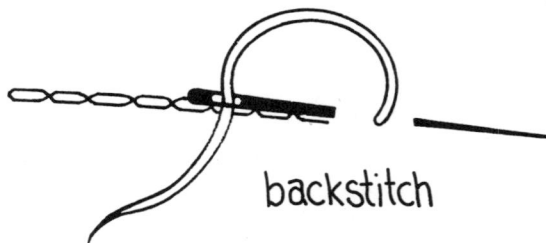

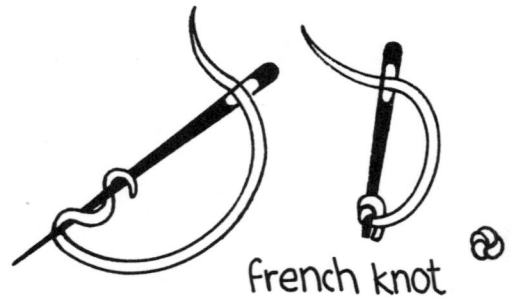

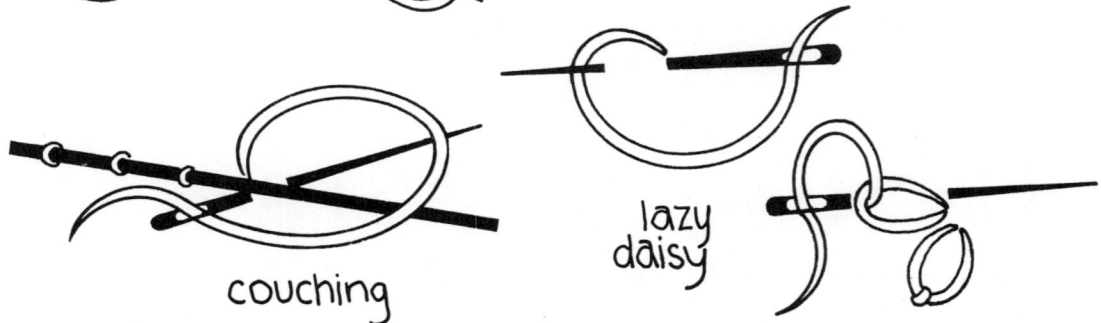

running stitch

overstitching

backstitch

chain stitch

french knot

couching

lazy daisy

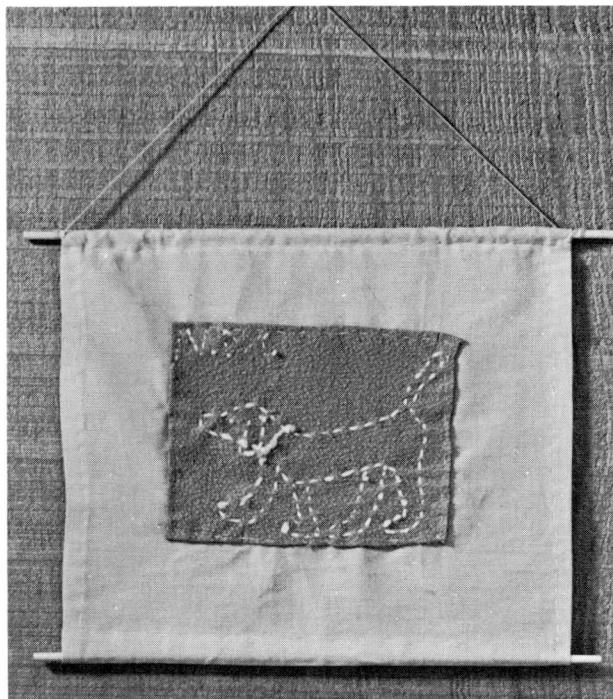

An embroidered dog picture

This picture of a happy dog taking a walk was made by an 8-year-old girl using her needle and yarn. For the dog's outline, she made **running stitches** on blue wool. She made an orange yarn collar using a **couching stitch**. Then she hemmed a piece of orange cloth, sewed it onto the picture, and put in dowels for hangers.

Two burlap wall hangings

Does the hippo in the picture below on the right look happy because of the three pretty flowers he has eaten? His smile, happy eyes, toenails, and the bright flowers in his tummy, as well as his greeting, "Hi", are made from **felt** glued with **rubber cement** to the burlap background. Use felt marking pens for outlining the body. For the border around the picture, use a **chain stitch**. In the picture below on the left a bright blue horse with a **daisy stitch** eye chats with a **chain stitch** snail. Make the load of flowers and the sun from cloth scraps and sew them on. Tie four clumps of **yarn** around a **dowel** and staple it to the bottom of the hanging. Attach another to the top.

Lion, mouse, and owl pincushions

Decorated with felt and yarn embroidery, these burlap pincushions make nice gifts. Each shape is a chopped-off triangle. Cut 2 **burlap** triangles which are about 6 inches wide at the bottom.

Both the lion and the mouse have **French knot** (see page 40) eyes, **felt** ears, and felt cheeks held in place with an **overstitch** from the outside to the center. The lion's whiskers and mouth and the outline of the owl's face are made with a **couching** stitch. The lion's ruff is made with yarn knots using double thread.

Sew the animals by hand or by machine and leave a hole in the top of each one for stuffing with cotton. Then sew up the holes, add fringed burlap to the stitch line and attach braided **yarn** tails.

Felt poppy pincushion

A bright orange poppy pincushion like the one shown below is a good place to keep your pins while you are sewing. To make it you will need orange, green, and black pieces of **felt** and a ball of **cotton** for stuffing. Cut a black felt circle, about 5 inches across, using a paper pattern pinned to the felt, as shown in the picture. Then cut 5 orange petals (with pinking shears if you have them) and one green leaf. Using needle and thread, sew a **running stitch** (see page 40) around the outside of the black circle, place a piece of cotton on it, pull the thread up tight to form a ball, and tie. Overlap the petals and sew them to the bottom of the black ball. Last of all, sew the green leaf to the bottom of the petals.

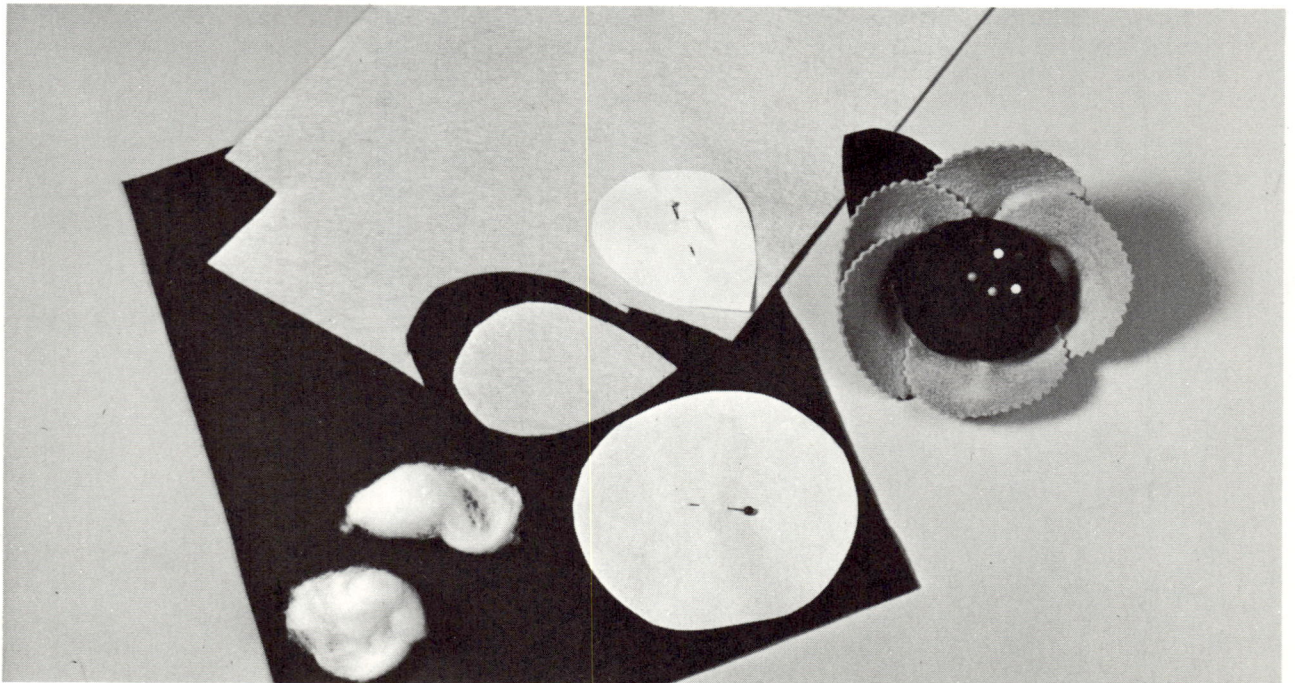

Easy burlap weaving

By pulling out a few threads across a piece of **burlap** and embroidering several rows of easy stitches using colorful **yarn,** you can have a wall hanging that looks hand woven. Start with a 10-by-12-inch piece of tan burlap. Measure down an inch from the top and start the first row of stitching. The last row of stitching should stop at least two inches from the bottom so there is room for fringing and a **dowel.** The dowel can be stapled or glued in place. To make this wall hanging, just follow the 10 easy steps listed below:

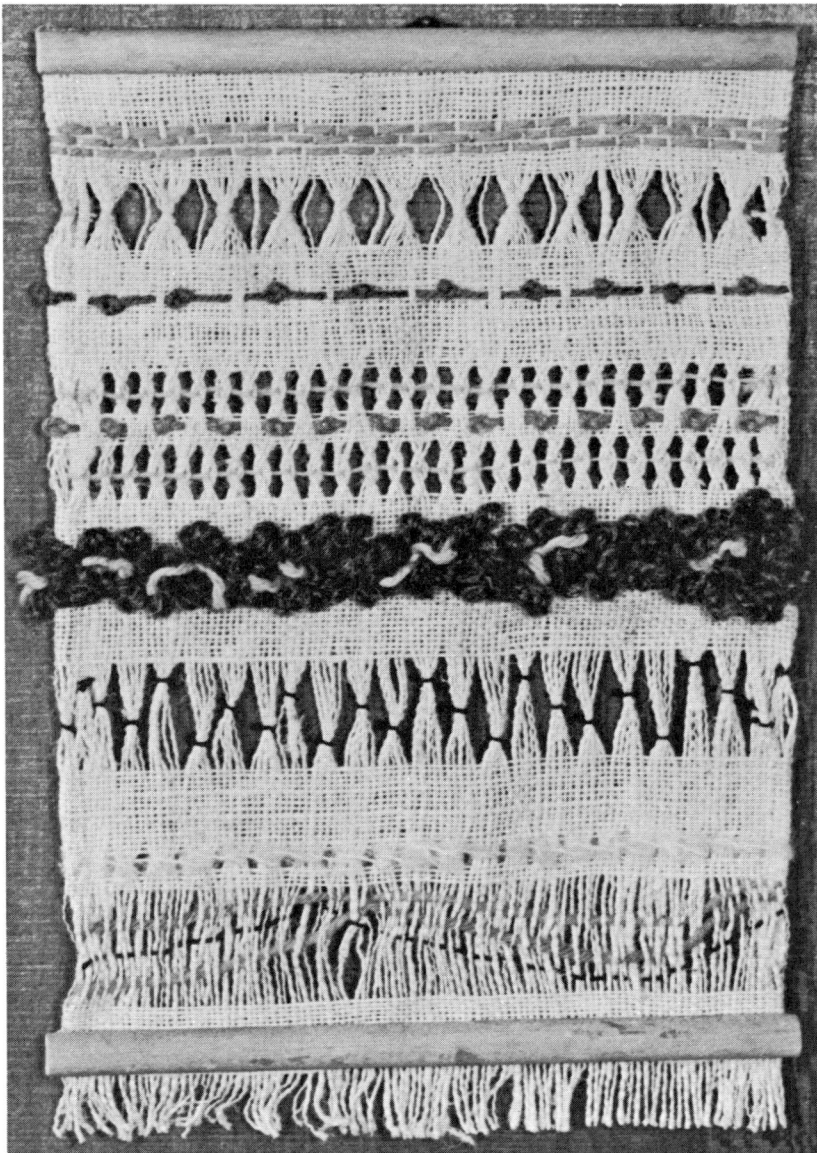

Step 1. Make three lines of **running stitches** (see page 40) using bright pink yarn.

Step 2. Pull out 15 rows of thread. Then tie bundles of 8 up-and-down threads together leaving 1 in the middle.

Step 3. Using brown yarn, make a line of **running stitches,** tying a big knot in the yarn before you push the needle back through.

Step 4. Pull out 10 rows of thread, twist bundles of 3 up-and-down threads, and run pink yarn through the centers using a **running stitch.**

Step 5. Using heavy green yarn, make a line of **running stitches,** tying a knot in the yarn before you push the needle back through.

Step 6. The same as step 4.

Step 7. Make **running stitches** for 2 lines. Do not pull the yarn all the way through on the top side. This makes the dark yarn look thick and furry. Tie loops together with yellow yarn.

Step 8. Pull out 20 rows of thread. Tie up-and-down threads into bundles of 5.

Step 9. Make a line of **back stitching** using fuzzy yellow yarn.

Step 10. Pull out 20 rows of thread. Weave in and out 3 lengths each of brown, pink, and green yarn.

Colorful batik pictures

Batik, which is pronounced **bah-teek**, is a Javanese way of making designs on cloth using hot wax and dye. It is definitely a craft to be supervised, or for older boys and girls. You paint a design on **cotton cloth** (an old sheet is good) with hot melted wax and then dip the cloth into fabric dye. The places you have waxed will not be colored by the dye. The sunflower batik shown on the right is a good project to start with. Try making it first, then experiment with other designs and colors. Blobs and streaks of hot wax brushed on in many patterns make batiks young children like—see photos above.

What to use. A square of **paraffin wax** placed in a large pan and then in a **pan of hot water**; a small **paintbrush**; fabric **dye** in packets or plastic bottles; **large jars** or enamel pans to mix the dye in; and many old **newspapers**.

How to do it. Cover the work area with newspapers. Using a piece of chalk or charcoal, lightly draw your design on a piece of cloth. Then, melt the wax, and follow the steps shown in the picture at right and on opposite page.

1. Brush melted wax completely around design and on spots in center of flower. Reheat wax to thin. The wax **must** go through to back of cloth.

2. Mix yellow dye in water, using package directions. Carefully dip the waxed fabric into the dye. Wear rubber gloves to protect hands.

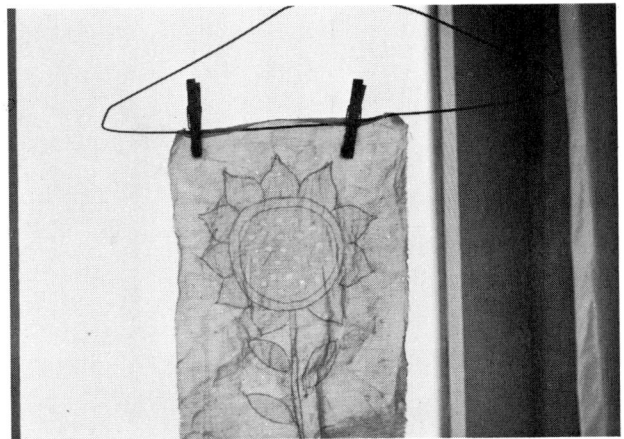

3. Rinse the cloth in clear water. Do **not** wring it. Hang it up to drip dry in the shade. The parts not waxed will be dyed yellow.

4. Put a second coat of **wax** on the places you want to **stay yellow**—part of blossom and center of leaves. Then dip the cloth in red dye.

5. Again rinse and let dry completely. The red dye over the yellow dye makes a lovely orange outline around petals, leaves, and flower center.

6. Put a third coat of wax on the places you want to stay orange. Mix some blue dye and re-dip the fabric. Rinse in clear water.

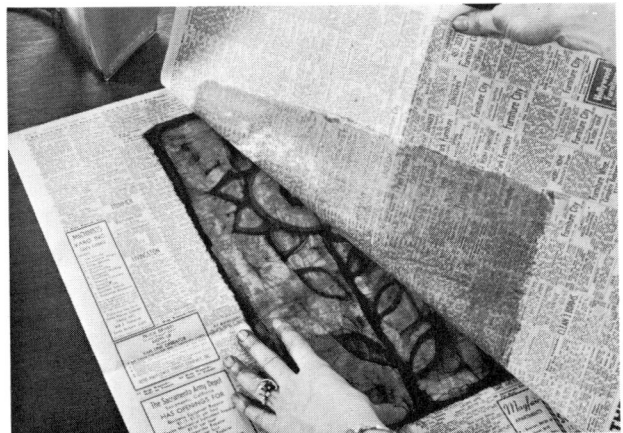

7. Place the wet fabric between newspapers or paper towels, then press with a hot iron until all of the wax is removed. The colors will be bright.

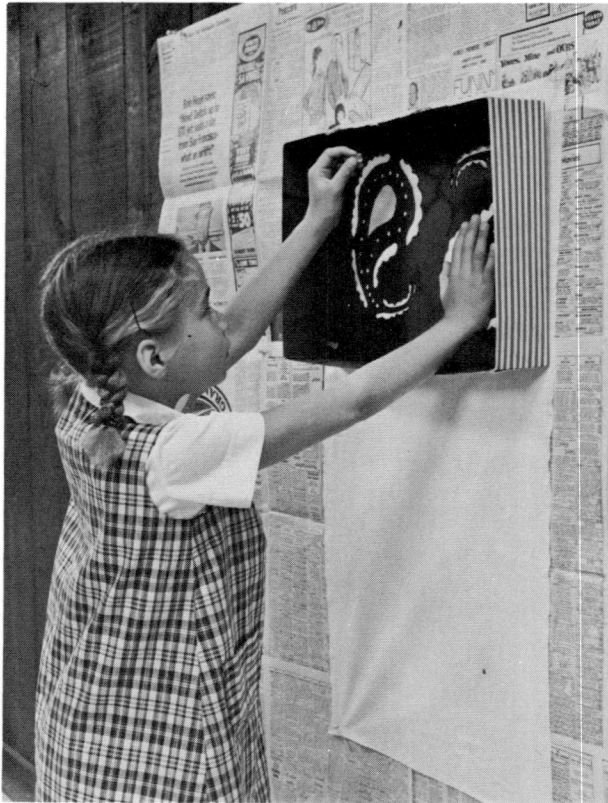

Spray paint stencil design

Colorful designs for curtains, bedspreads, or other large pieces of cloth can be printed quickly using a stencil cut in the top of a coat box and a can of **fabric spray paint.**

Draw the design in the **box top** and cut it out with a **craft knife.** On the piece of **cloth** (unbleached muslin is a good choice) lightly mark each place where the design is to be printed. Pin the cloth to an outside or garage wall that is protected with newspaper. Using **thumbtacks,** pin the stencil in place over the cloth.

Holding the can of paint about 10 inches from the stencil, spray to fill in the design. Instead of holding the can in one place, move it back and forth so the paint will be even. Remove the stencil, clean it well with **paper towels,** and pin it in the next position.

Again, spray the paint to fill in the design, remove and clean the stencil, and fasten it to the next place. Repeat these steps until you have printed the design all over the cloth. Hem the fabric only after it is completely dry.

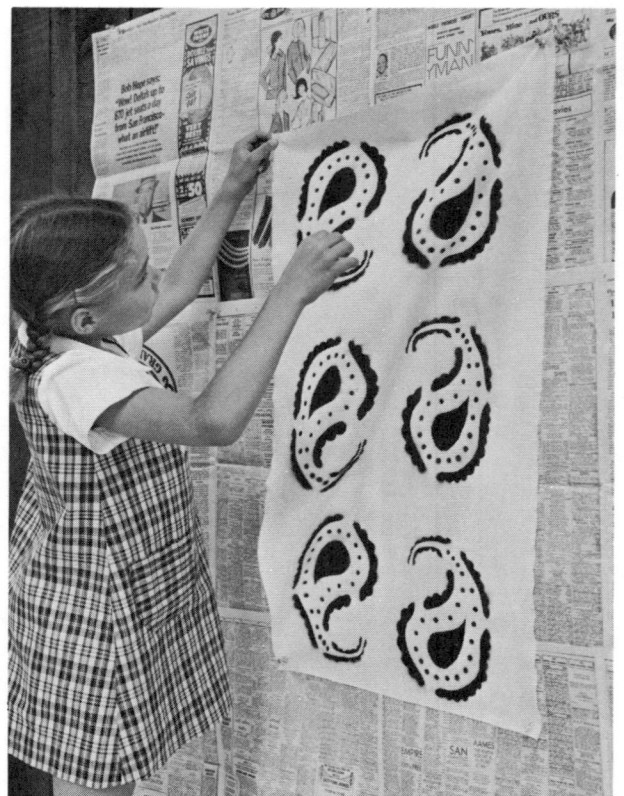

Iron-on designs

A pair of gaily decorated gloves is always a welcome gift for a mother or grandmother who likes to garden. Because they are quick and easy to make, this is a good project for Cub Scouts and Brownies or Bluebirds. Buy **iron-on fabric tape** in blue, red, and yellow. Cut out 10 red fingernails, and yellow and blue blossoms for each pair **of gloves.** Press on the designs with a hot **iron.**

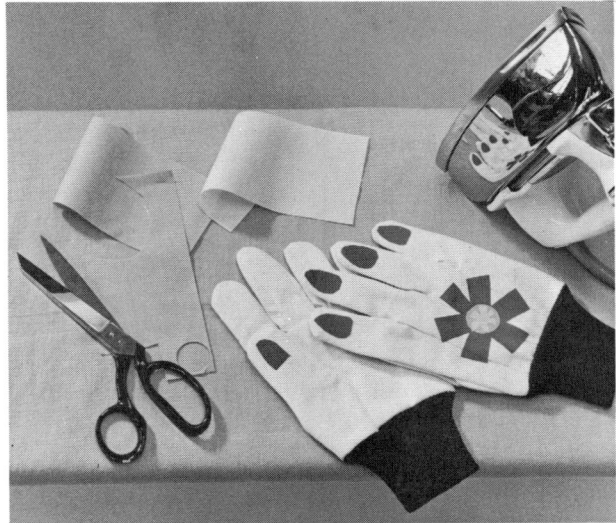

Cheerful pillowcase pictures

These unusual pillowcases can be made by creating designs with **felt marking pens.** Using a pencil, copy pictures you like or lightly draw your design on a plain white **pillowcase.** Then use various shades of marking pens to color the design. The colors are permanent and will not wash out. You can also use felt pens to decorate canvas sneakers, jeans, and bike bags.

Crayon designs on cloth

Children of all ages have good ideas for making **crayon** designs on things made of cloth—place mats, curtains, chair back covers, or scarfs. Trace the design on the cloth, and fill in with crayons. Make the design permanent by pressing the cloth with a hot **iron.** If needed, outline the design with a **felt marking pen.**

WOOD CRAFTS

NAIL PICTURE • HOUSE SIGN • WOOD & PAPER PICTURES
COLLECTION DISPLAYS • TIC-TAC-TOE BOARD • PENCIL HOLDER • STILTS
BALSA WOOD PINS & CONSTRUCTIONS • KITES

House sign made of wood scraps

For the background of this house sign you need one piece of **plywood** or other wood about 6 inches wide and 12 inches long. Using enamel or acrylic **paint**, mix a color you like and paint the board on the front and sides. When the paint is completely dry, measure 5 inches across from the left side and then trace your house numbers. Use bright colored paint to fill in these numbers (you can also outline them with another color). Then gather up odd sizes and shapes of wood and **glue** or nail them to the right front section. Paint each piece of wood you have added and then make a hanger for the back using a bent **nail** or **wire**.

Nail and yarn picture

To make this apple tree picture you will need a piece of **wood** about 8 inches wide and 10 inches long. **Sandpaper** the edges until they are smooth and paint the wood with **white paint** (spray paint, enamel, acrylic, or poster paint). Then, put some **brown paint** on a cloth and rub it lightly into any nicks and holes and along the edges. This makes the wood look old and is called "antiquing". Lightly draw the outline of the tree on the dry wood. Along the outline, **hammer** in nails about halfway into the board (use 1-inch, round head **brass brads)**. To make the branches, hammer several more nails on the inside of the outline. Then wind **brown yarn** around the top of each nail, following the shape of the tree and in and out of the branches. Make apples by winding red or yellow yarn many times around some of the nails. Add a **ring hanger** and the picture is ready.

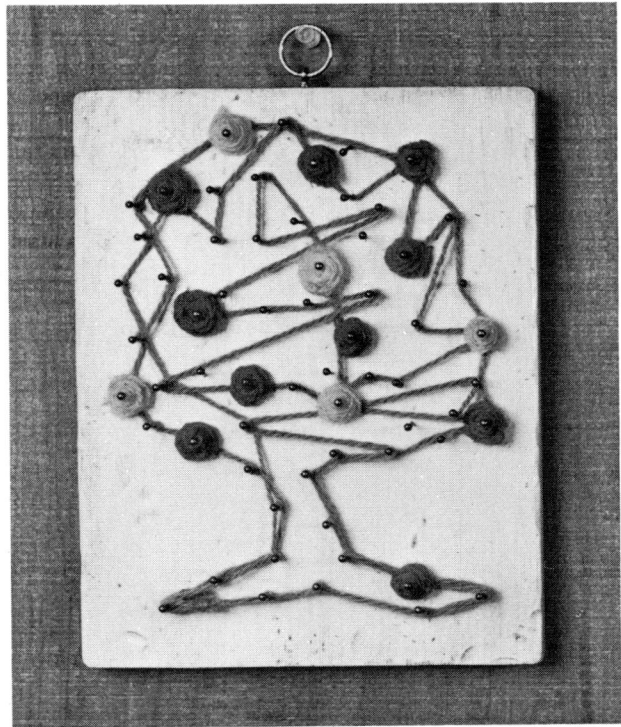

HOW TO USE BASIC WOODWORKING TOOLS

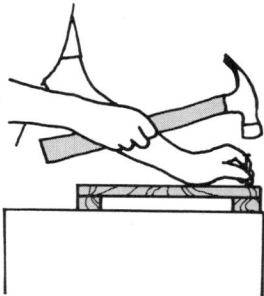

To hammer a nail, hold the nail firmly on the wood and with a hammer pound it straight down.

To saw wood, place the saw on your mark and pull toward you. Then saw slowly and evenly.

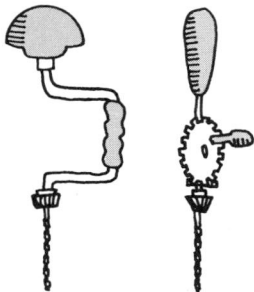

To bore a hole, use a hand drill for neat, small holes. For holes bigger than a quarter inch across, you will need a brace and bit. After placing the tip of the bit on the mark you have made, keep the drill or brace and bit straight up and down. Crank the handle with smooth, even turns.

Magazine picture plaques

Choose a colorful picture from an old magazine to use for making your plaque (a French word for plate). Cut a piece of **wood** big enough to frame the picture. Using **white glue**, paste down the picture in the center of the frame. To antique your plaque like the two shown above, dip a cloth into **dark paint** and carefully rub it all over the wood and onto the edges of the picture. When the paint is dry, screw a **metal hanger** into the top of the plaque.

Collections mounted on wood blocks

A good way to display a small stamp, ring, key, shell, or button collection is to mount it on little wood blocks. The stamp collection shown below on the left was mounted on pieces of wood cut from **pine molding**. The edges were curved using **sandpaper**, the blocks were painted a dark color, and **brass hangers** were added. The key collection shown below on the right side was mounted on molding blocks that had been painted white. **White glue** was used to attach the keys, but hanging them on tiny screw hooks would work equally as well.

A wooden pencil holder

Even short pencils are quite easy to reach in this holder. You will need a block of **wood** about 4 inches square. Using a **drill** or brace and bit, make 16 holes equal spaces apart which go almost to the bottom of the block. (Be sure to use a drill that makes a hole bigger than your pencils.) Saw off the top of the block at an angle so that the front is 2-1/2 inches high. Then **sandpaper** the sides, top, and around the holes. **Paint** the holder or rub it with **floor wax**.

Tic-tac-toe board

A tic-tac-toe board is a handy game to take traveling. This one is made from wood with paper designs glued to the top. Cut a piece of **plywood** or other wood about 8 inches square and **sandpaper** the edges. Using **construction paper** and **felt pens**, make 9 designs to fit the 9 squares used in the game. **Paste down** the designs and cover the front of the board with clear **contact paper**. Make the crosses and circles from paper.

Stilts...how to make them, how to use them

With some help from your dad and your friends, you can make enough stilts for the whole neighborhood in a very short time. If you make the stilts in different heights, everyone will have fun trading back and forth. Walking on stilts is really a matter of shifting your weight from side to side while you lift and hold onto each pole. If you need some help getting started, use short stilts and have someone stand behind you to hold the pole tops until you get going. The directions on the next page tell you how to make stilts like the ones shown in the pictures here.

What to use. Stilts for young boys and girls can be made from standard **1- by 2-inch lumber** cut in lengths of 5 to 7 feet. If you want to make taller stilts, you will need wood that is 2 inches square. To make a footblock, you need a piece of **2- by 4-inch lumber**, **glue**, and **hammer** and **nails**. **Sandpaper** the footblock to avoid getting splinters. You will also need a **saw**.

How to make them. Cut the poles to the size you want. Next, cut a 6-inch-long footblock from the 2- by 4-inch lumber and make a slanting cut on it as shown in the drawing below. Using glue, fasten the long side of the footblock to the pole at the height you want. Then turn the stilt around and hammer 4 or 5 nails through the pole and into the footblock. Be sure that the footblocks are attached at the same height on both stilts.

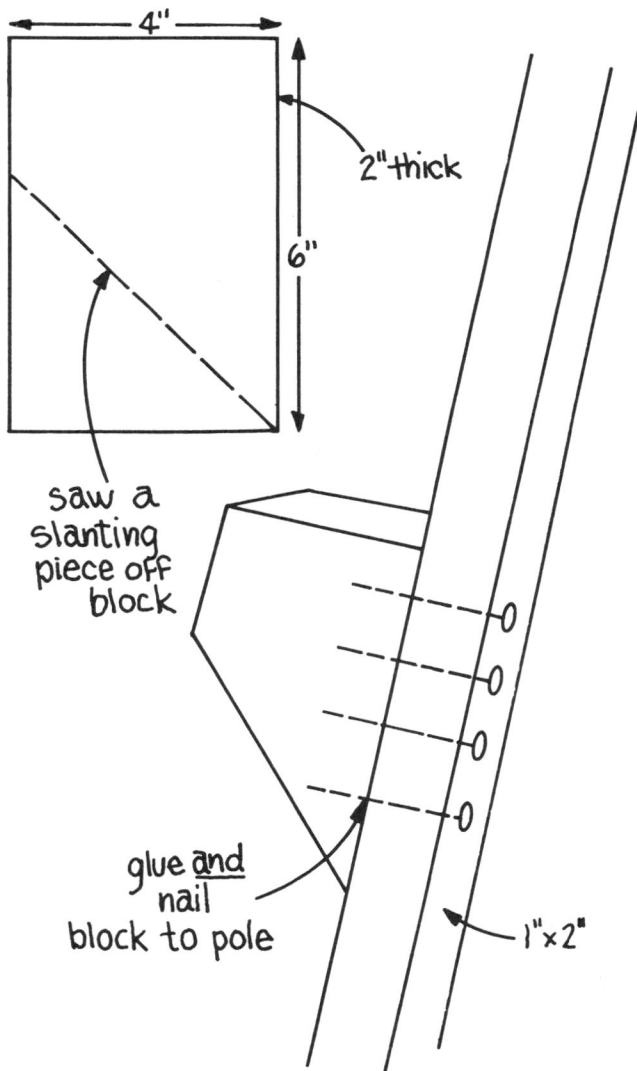

4"

2" thick

6"

saw a
slanting
piece off
block

glue and
nail
block to pole

1" x 2"

A three-stick kite

When the fresh spring winds blow, you and your friends will want to get out to an open field and fly your kites. Part of the fun of kite flying is making your own kite. A standard three-stick kite is easy to build. It is also a good flyer.

How to do it. You need three 1/2-inch dowels or thin wood **sticks**, newsprint or some other thin **paper** for covering, **string**, scraps of **cloth**, and **white glue.** Cross two 36-inch-long dowels and a third one 30 inches long (see A, B, and C in the drawing on the right). Tie them together at the center joint. Cut a notch in both ends of each stick and stretch string between the notches to outline the shape of the kite. Wrap string around the ends of the sticks to keep them from splitting (see drawing). Lay the frame on the paper and draw an outline 2 inches bigger than the frame. Then fold the paper over the string and glue it in place. Fasten a length of string from one end of stick A to the other end. Fasten two other strings between the ends of sticks B and C. At the point where these three strings cross, fasten a ball of string for flying the kite. For a tail, tie a length of string between the ends of sticks A and B and at the center point fasten a 36-inch string to which cloth strips have been tied.

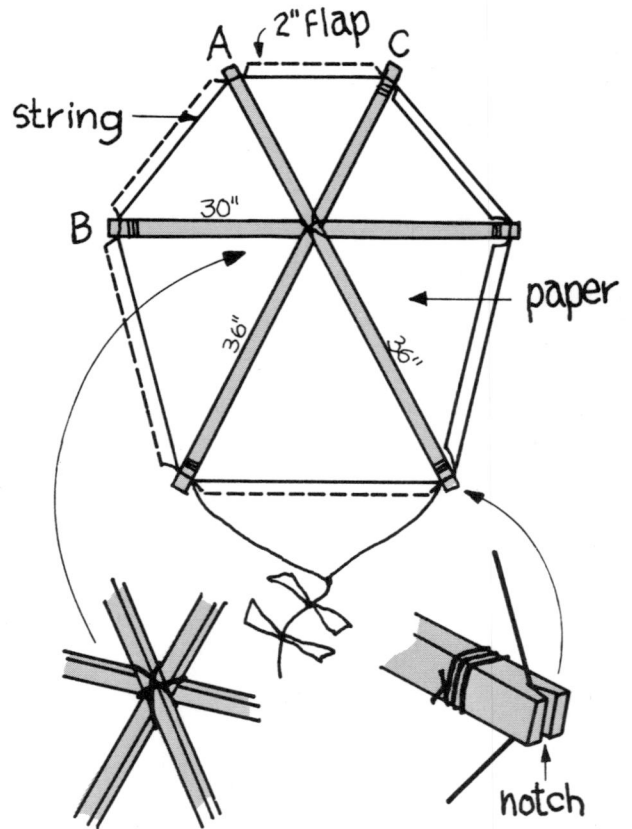

A hawk kite

Although the easy diamond-shaped two and three stick kites are the best known, you can make a kite in almost any form. This kite is made in the shape of a hawk.

How to do it. You will need three thin **bamboo strips.** Soak them in water for an hour so they will bend easily into the shapes shown in the picture at right. Securely tie the strips with **heavy thread** as shown in the top picture on the right. Put the tied frame on **tissue paper** and draw an outline that is slightly larger than the frame. Then cut out the paper pattern, fold the edges over the bamboo strips, and glue them down with **white glue.** Do not cover the wing tips.

Using **poster paint** or ink, draw a hawk design as shown in the picture on the right. Tie a length of thread between the wing tips making it tight enough to draw the wings up into a bow shape. Then cut three lengths of thread, each about a foot long, and tie two of them to the front edges of the wings and one to the tail. Fasten the loose ends of the three threads together and attach the kite string. Add a string tail with cloth strips to the hawk's tail.

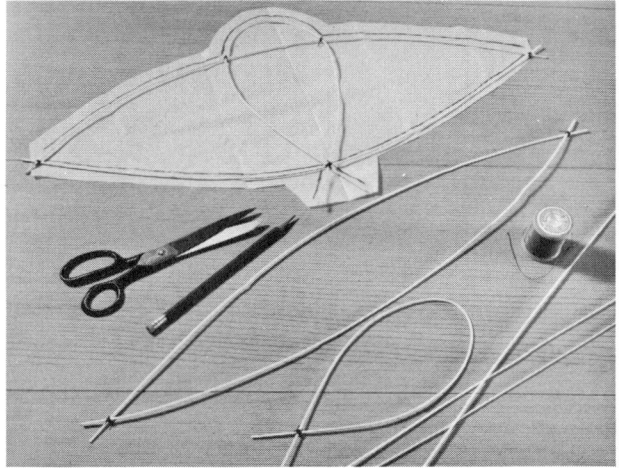

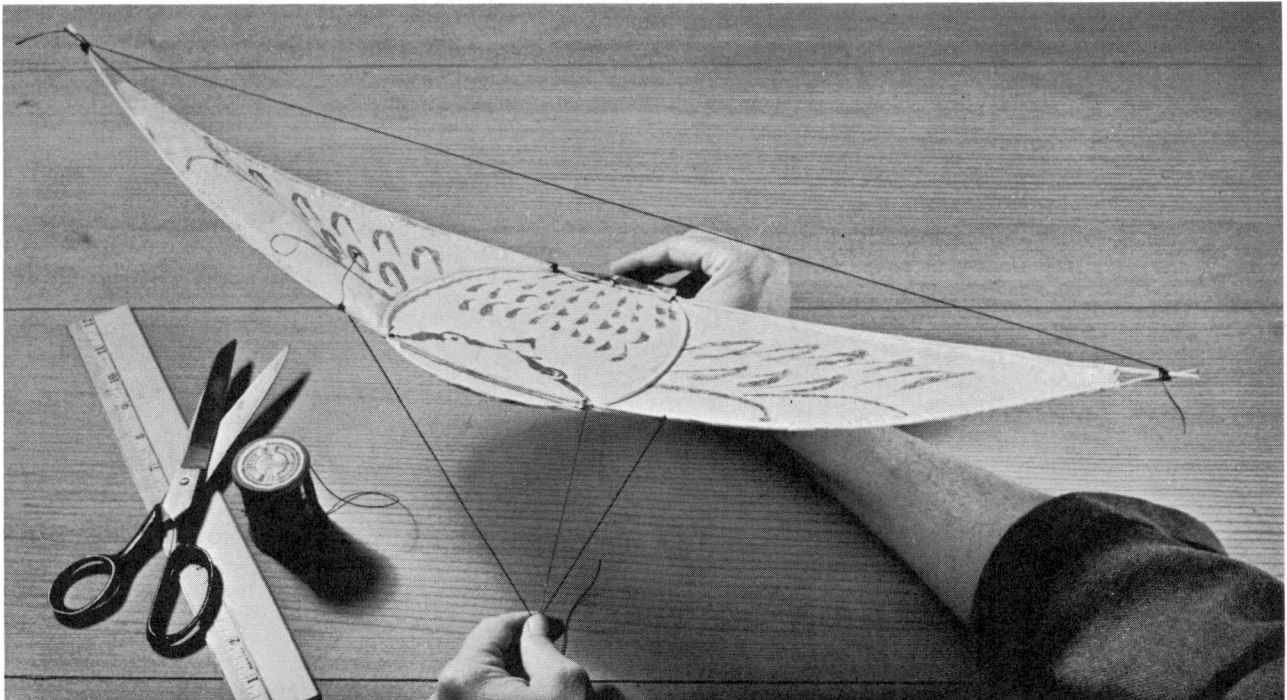

Building with Balsa Wood

The projects shown below and on the opposite page are made with balsa wood—the lightest wood in the world and also one of the strongest. A piece of cork the same size as a piece of balsa wood weighs four times more. You can cut thin pieces of balsa using a craft knife or scissors. It can easily be glued together to make a strong construction, and it is a beautiful pale, tan color.

A construction made from balsa strips

The construction shown below is made from small and narrow strips of **balsa wood.** First, cover the table with several layers of **newspapers** to protect it from being cut. A good way to start your construction is to fasten three long strips of balsa together tepee style using **a straight pin.** (If you keep a number of pins stuck into a bar of soap, it will be easier to put them into the balsa). Cut and pin each strip in place until the construction is balanced and it pleases you. Then use **white glue** to hold the parts firmly in place. When the glue is completely dry, remove the pins.

A window of balsa strips and tissue paper

Bright sunlight shining through colored tissue paper on this balsa wood panel makes it look like a stained glass window. It can be made to fit into a window or to hang in front of one so that the light will make the colors glow. This panel is 8 inches wide and 15 inches long. The frame and most of the inside pieces are 1/4-inch balsa but some are 1/8-inch.

How to do it. Place a large sheet of **wax paper** on your work table to keep the glued parts of the project from sticking to the table. Cut and lay out strips of the balsa wood in the shape you wish. Glue them together with **white glue**, using **straight pins** to hold the strips in place until the glue dries. Cut colored **tissue paper** a little bigger than the sections of the frame and attach them on the back with glue.

Big balsa brooches

Clocks, daisies, apples, leaves—even bugs are all good subjects for making big brooches from balsa wood that is a quarter inch thick. Whatever design you choose, be sure to keep it very simple. Copy the design on the wood and cut it out using a **craft knife. Sandpaper** the edges of the brooch until they are smooth. Then paint with **poster paint** and spray on a coat of **shellac.** In the picture at right, the clock has heavy **colored paper** hands fastened to its face with a brass **tack.** The numbers are painted a different color. A cluster of short, round-headed **pins** is used to make the center of the flower brooch. A **clasp** from a hobby shop is glued to the back of each brooch.

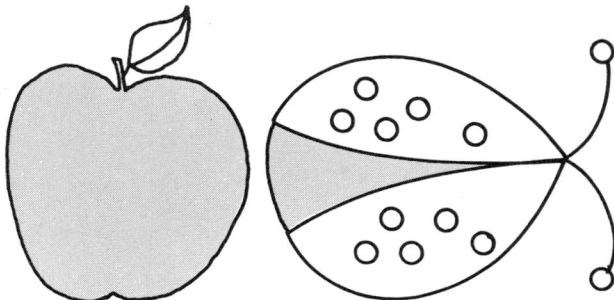

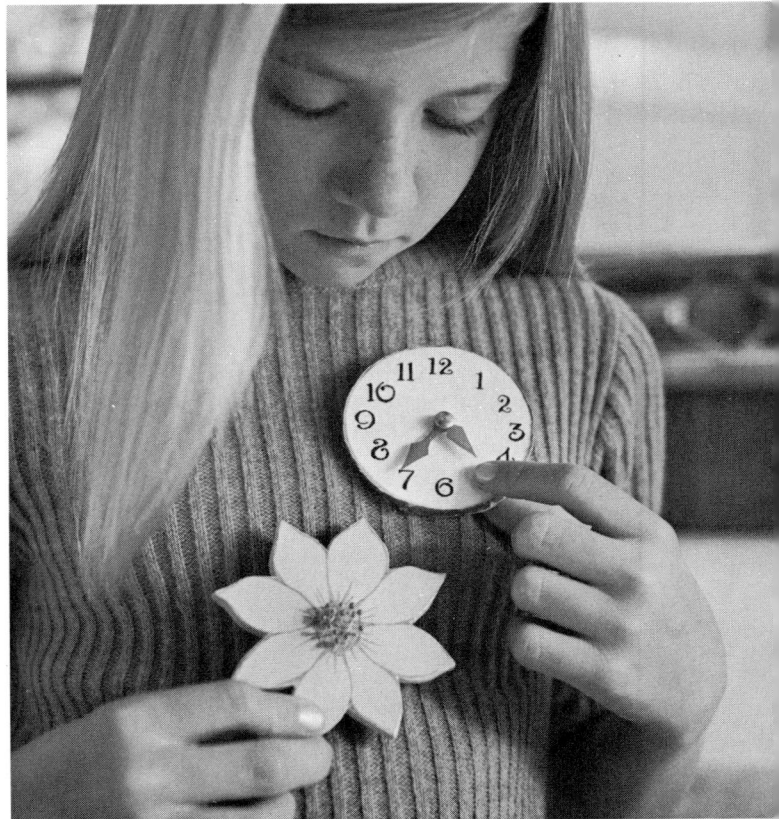

CERAMICS, MOSAICS, AND PLASTER CRAFTS

CERAMIC PENDANTS & ANIMAL MOBILES • CANDLEHOLDERS
BIG BUG PAPERWEIGHT • CLAY-DOUGH DECORATIONS
MOSAIC HOT PAD & PICTURES • JUNK MOSAIC • FLOWER POT RIM
SEED MOSAICS • SCRIMSHAW • PLASTER PRINTS • SAND CASTS

GENERAL INSTRUCTIONS FOR WORKING WITH CLAY

The ceramic projects shown on the first few pages of this chapter are made with a water-base clay—the kind that will harden by itself or in your mother's oven. You can buy this clay at any craft store. Be sure to ask for baking or hardening directions.

Keep clay in a plastic container which has a tight fitting lid until you are ready to begin your project. This will keep it moist and easy to work. (If the clay starts to harden while you are working on your project, just add a little water squeezed from a sponge. Or, dampen your fingers while you are working.) Your hands are the main tools you will need, but sticks, buttons, and forks are also useful for making designs.

Pat and poke the clay until it is very soft before you begin making your project. Use a piece of plastic or oil cloth to protect the work table and keep the clay from sticking to it. Cover any unfinished work with a damp cloth or plastic to keep the clay soft. When you have finished a project, follow the directions for baking or hardening the clay. Then paint your project with poster paint. Special ceramic glazes can be used but **only** if you have the use of a kiln (a special oven which has a very high heat for drying this type of glaze).

Slab method. The pendants shown on the opposite page and the hanging ceramic animals on page 60 are made with the slab method of working clay. This means to pat a ball of clay until it is evenly flattened—or roll it out using a piece cut from an old broom handle, a dowel, or an old rolling pin. Then, cut out the shape and make the design. Let it harden before painting.

Ball method. The paperweight and the simple candleholders on page 61 are made with the ball method. Pinch off a ball of clay the size you want and smooth it with your fingers and hands. Stick the balls of clay together with a little more clay moistened with water. Then, scratch in the decoration you want. Let the project harden before painting it.

Coil method. Here is another easy method of working with clay. Roll a ball of clay between your hands or on a flat surface until it becomes long and snake-shaped. The wreath, candy-cane, and tree on page 62 are made with the coil method.

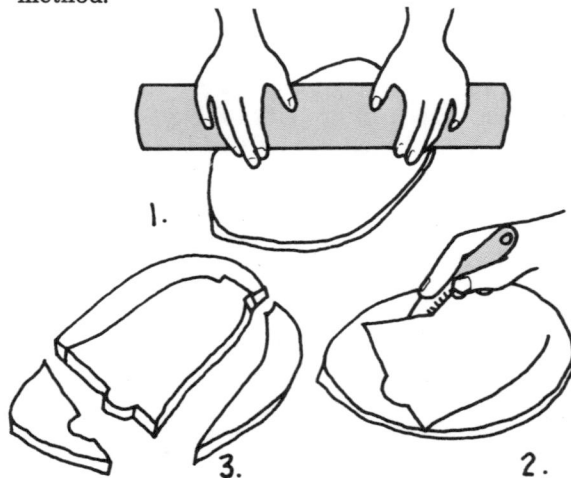

Pendant in the shape of an owl

Designs with birds, leaves or flowers — anything that has a simple shape—are effective to use for making ceramic pendants. Roll out a small slab of **clay** until it is a quarter-inch-thick. Cut out an owl shape about as big as a 50-cent piece and poke a hole in the top for attaching a **leather thong** or a length of **yarn.** Use a **stick** to make the feathers and beak. For eyes, use tiny **glass beads** pressed into the clay. Allow the pendant to harden completely before wearing it.

Round pendants

These round pendants are about the easiest ceramic projects you can make. First, roll out a slab of clay about a quarter inch thick. Place a small glass on the clay and trace around it with a toothpick. Then, using a knife cut out the circle along the tracing line. Punch a hole in the top for a cord. The names and decorations on two of the pendants were made with a pointed stick. The leaf design on the third pendant was made by pressing an old earring into the clay. The pendants were glazed and dried in a kiln, but you could also paint them with poster paint and shellac.

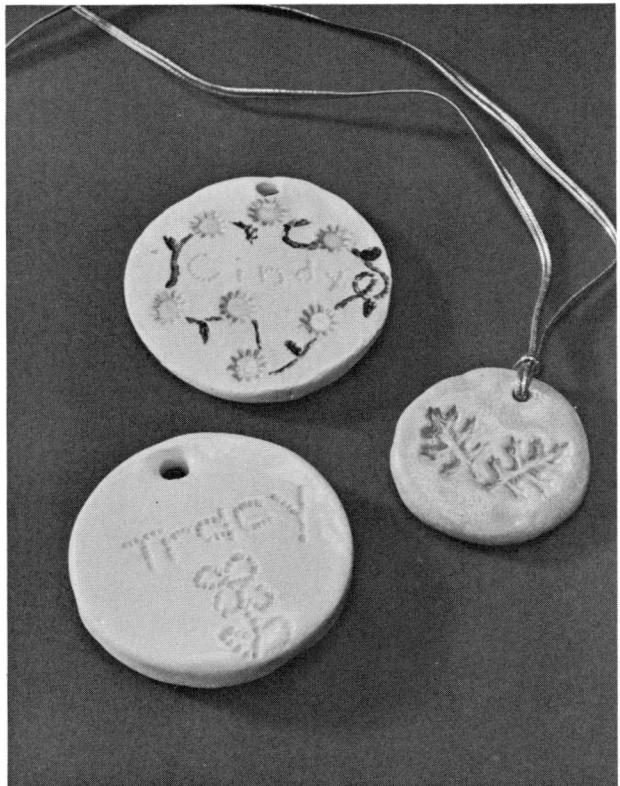

Ceramic animals that can move

These delightful ceramic animals—a lion and a raccoon—nod their heads and even wag their tails. Both are cut out from a slab of light-colored **clay** about a half inch thick. Cut separate pieces for the heads, bodies, and the raccoon's tail. Using a **knitting needle,** punch holes through each piece from top to bottom. Dry, then paint with **poster paints** (or glaze and dry in a kiln). String a **leather thong** through the holes in each figure, leaving a top loop and making a heavy knot at the bottom.

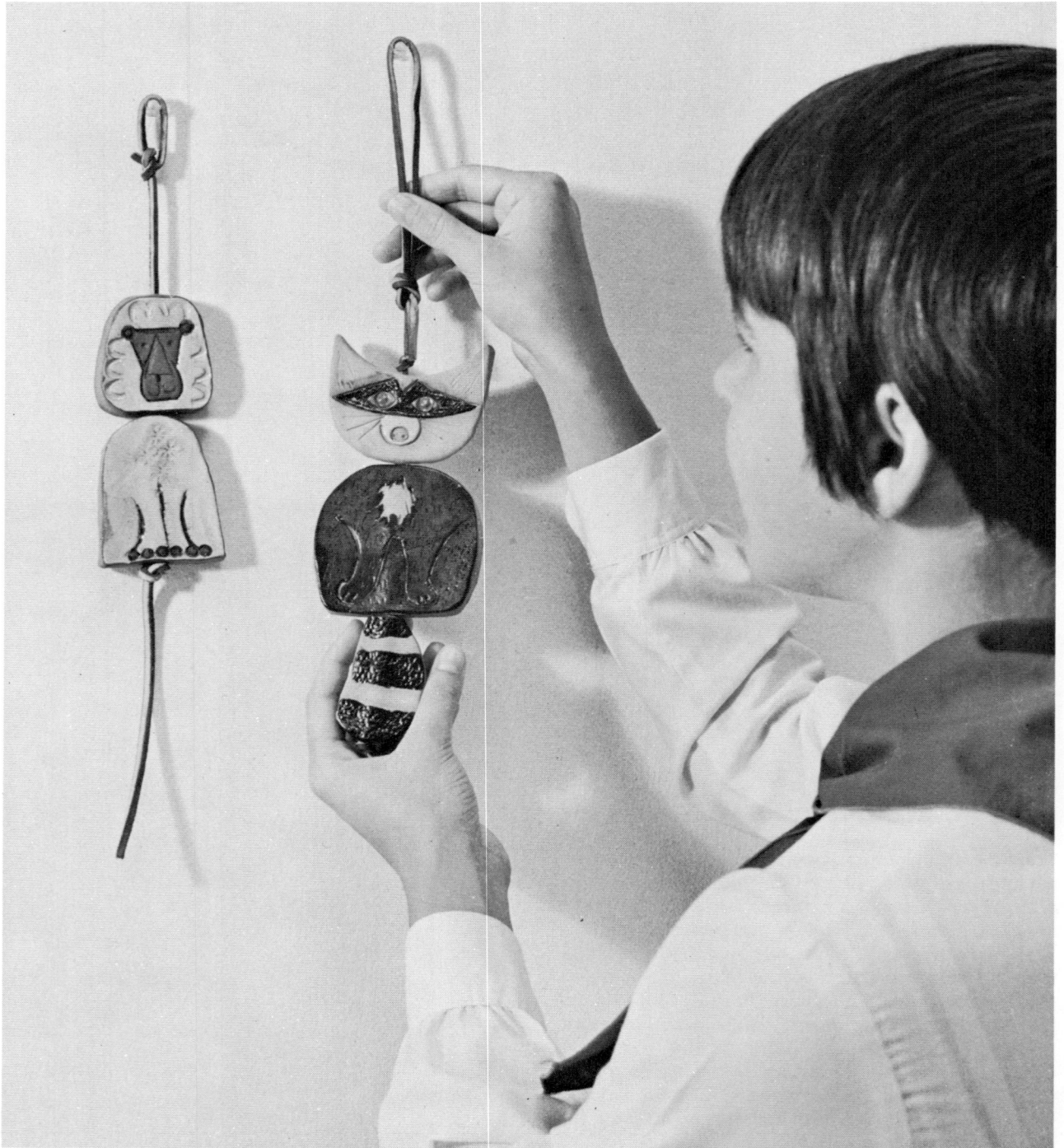

A pair of simple candleholders

A pair of candleholders is a delightful gift for any occasion. Roll a piece of **clay** between your hands until it is in the shape of a ball about the size of a small orange. Then whack it down on your work table to flatten the bottom. Using your thumb, press a hole in the center about an inch deep and put a **candle** into the hole to see if it fits. Make designs with a **stick** and let the clay harden before painting.

Big bug paperweight

This big, bright green bug is formed from three lumps of **clay**, each one about the size of a golf ball. One at a time, roll the balls between your hands until they are smooth. For wings, attach two balls together using a little clay moistened with water. For the head, attach the third ball of clay in the same way. To make a base, press the bug against the table until the bottom is flat. Punch holes for the eyes with a **pencil**. When the bug is completely dry, **paint** it with bright colors. Then brush on a **shellac**.

Clay-dough ornaments

Made from flour and salt dough, these Christmas decorations are then baked in the oven. This dough mixture (called clay-dough) works as well as clay for making small projects.

How to make clay-dough. Mix 1 cup flour, 1/2 cup **salt,** and **water** (about 1/2 cup) to make a stiff mixture. Bake the finished ornaments in a 225° oven for several hours, turning them over frequently to keep them from curling.

How to make the tree ornaments. On a floured board, roll out the dough using a **rolling pin.** Cut out the shapes with a **knife** or **cookie cutter.** You can also mold the dough, roll it into strips, or braid it. Make a hole in the top of each ornament for hanging. Then, bake in the oven on a **cooky sheet.** Paint with **poster paint** which has been mixed wih a little **white glue** to keep it from flaking. Make a wooden tree from four **dowels** tied together. For the tree base, cut a block of **wood** about 4 inches wide, 8 inches long, and 2 inches thick. In the center, drill a hole and glue the tree in place.

Make the figures for the Christmas scene shown below in the same way.

Working with Mosaics

Mosaics are pictures or decorations made by fitting together small pieces of mosaic tile, linoleum, rocks, or paper into a pleasing design. You can also use other things, such as beans, seeds, and bottle caps. The background for your design can be a piece of ceramic tile, a board, a tray, or a flowerpot. White glue is used to hold the design pieces in place, and **grout** (fine cement mixed with water) is used for filling cracks and holes. (Mosaic tiles and grout can be purchased at a craft store.)

Paper mosaic picture

The tulip design in this mosaic was made with squares of red and green construction paper. The squares were glued to a background of bright yellow paper. For the frame, a dark and slightly bigger piece of paper was used. It is a good idea to always save unusual pieces of paper for mosaics—scraps of gold or silver or especially heavy paper. Paint color sample cards from a paint store are excellent, too.

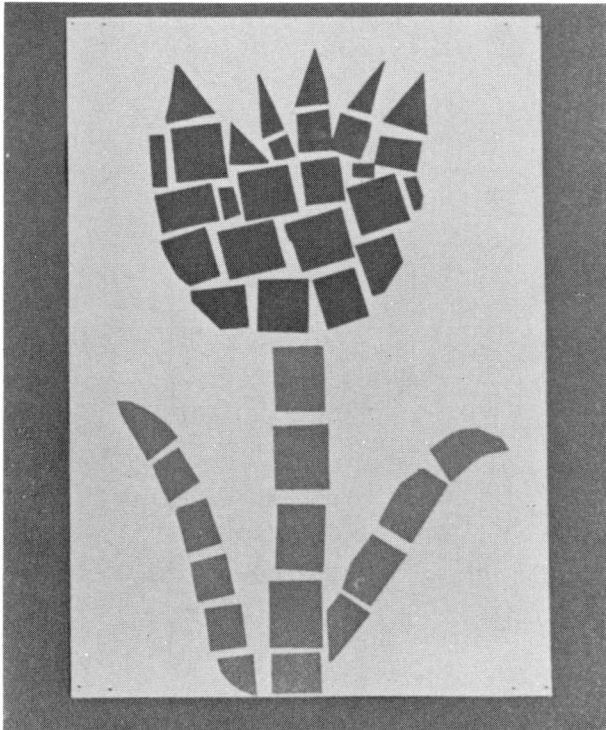

Mosaic tile hot pad

You can make this handy, shiny hot pad using a hundred and forty-four tiny, mosaic tiles (each less than a half inch square). White, tan, brown, gray, and orange tiles were used in this design. Place the tiles on a 6-inch square **plastic tile** or smooth **board** in a pattern you like. Then **glue** them down. When the glue is dry, fill the cracks with **grout** and wipe the mosaic clean with a damp **cloth**. Glue **felt** to the bottom of the pad.

Linoleum mosaic picture

This unusual figure with pointed ears was made with small pieces of linoleum tiles glued to a piece of **plywood**. Using a **pencil**, copy this design (or one of your own) onto the board. Then cut the linoleum into rectangles to fit the design. **Glue** down the linoleum tiles. When the glue is dry, fill the open spaces and cracks with **grout**. Clean well with a damp **cloth**.

A junk mosaic

Big, red-spotted **beans**, white beans, curly and wheel-shaped **macaroni**, a few **glass beads**, three **corks**, and six **bottle caps** were used to make this picture of a flower basket. With the help of your mother, you can probably find the same kinds of odds and ends to make your own "junk mosaic". First, **paint** a **board** the color you like. When the paint is dry, plan your design and trace the outline onto the board. Then fill the outline with a thick coat of **white glue** and put the beans, corks, and other things in place. When the glue is completely dry, the picture is ready to hang up.

Mosaic rims on flower pots

Small pots for flowers are very pretty when the rims are decorated with tiny **mosaic tiles**. First, brush a coat of **white paint** over the rim and let it dry completely. Then, brush **glue** on the back of each tile and put it in place. When you have finished making your design and the glue is dry, fill the cracks with **grout**. Clean the mosaic with a damp **cloth**. After the grout has dried, you can fill the pots with dirt and put in little plants.

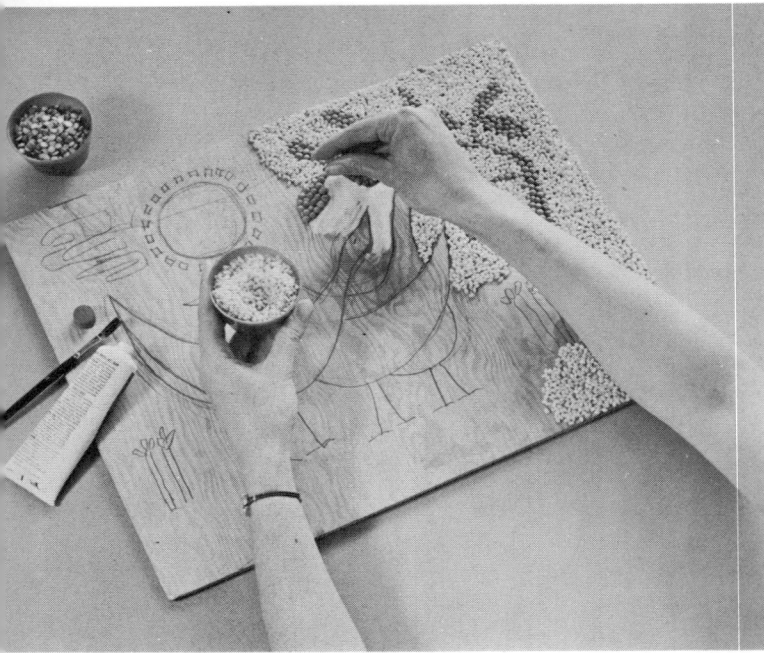

Mosaic pictures made with seeds

Making a seed mosaic is a very good project for the whole family because it takes a long time to complete—especially if you choose small seeds and a big design.

What to use. You need a **plywood board** on which to make your mosaic. Use **seeds** of any kind—rice, beans, split peas, bird seed, pumpkin, caraway, barley, and others that your mother may have in her kitchen. **Shallow dishes** are handy for keeping the seeds separate. You will also need **white glue**.

How to do it. First, plan your design. Remember that simple designs are usually the best. (In the picture below, the plain shapes of the bottles stand out very well against the white seeds on the background.) Then draw your design on the plywood. Brush white glue over a small area of the design and fill the space with seeds. In the same way, put on more glue and seeds until the picture is completely filled in.

Working with Plaster

Crafts that are made with plaster of Paris are fun to do because you can mix the plaster with water and pour it into a mold where it hardens quickly. Then it can be carved into various shapes or designs. For mixing the plaster, use a shallow plastic pan because it can be easily cleaned. Follow the directions on the box of plaster or use this recipe: Slowly pour 1 cup of plaster into 2/3 cup of water, stirring the mixture gently with your fingers until it is well mixed. Allow it to stand for one minute—no longer. (Plaster begins to harden, or "set up," very fast.) Then pour the plaster into molds, cartons, or into puddles on wax paper.

Funny flowers

These twisted, funny looking little flowers are made by winding bright colored, soft **electronic wire** around your finger or a pencil. You can buy this wire at a hardware store. After you have made the flowers, mix some **plaster** and pour it into a small **mold** or container such as a baking pan. Then, as the plaster begins to harden, push the stems of the flowers into the mixture. When the plaster is dry, remove the flowers and base from the mold.

Sand casts for plaster fish

By using scooped out damp sand as a mold, you can make these plaster fish in a backyard sandbox or at the beach. This craft is called sand casting.

What to use. You need about 5 pounds of **plaster of Paris** and a coffee **can** to mix it in. You also need **damp sand. Rocks, shells,** and **driftwood** can be used as decorations. To make plaster cast fish, follow the steps shown in the pictures below.

1. Using your hands, scoop out wet sand to make a mold that is about 6 inches wide, 12 inches long, and 2 inches deep.

2. While the sand is still damp, press shells, rocks, and driftwood, into the bottom of the mold. Poke holes to make spikes on the fish.

3. Fill the can 2/3 full of water and add plaster until it mounds up above the water. Stir with your hand and wait five minutes before pouring.

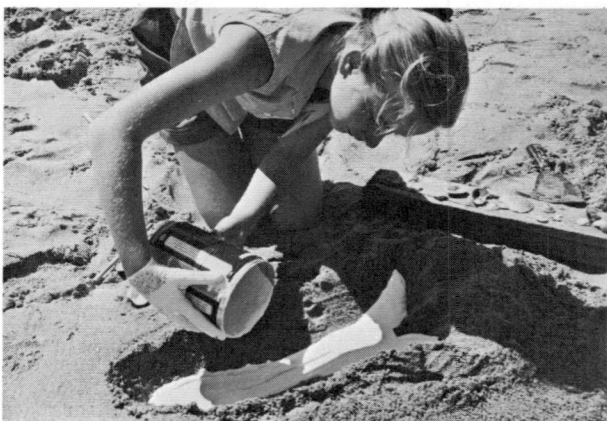

4. Carefully pour the plaster into the mold. Let it harden for an hour. Lift the fish out of the mold and brush off the loose sand.

Imitation scrimshaw

Scrimshaw is what early New England sailors called carvings made from whale bones. A good craft for a group, imitation scrimshaw can be made this way: Pour a blob of fresh **plaster** on **wax paper**. For a pendant, make a hole in the top. When dry, scratch Eskimo designs on it. Darken the lines with a **felt pen** or give the whole scrimshaw a wash with **poster paint**. **Varnish** for a shiny, bone-like look.

Printing with plaster blocks

Your favorite drawings can often be copied on plaster blocks and then printed on paper for Christmas or other greeting cards.

What to use. In a **plastic pan**, mix 1 cup of **plaster** with 2/3 cup of **water**. The mold is made from a cardboard **box top** coated with **petroleum jelly** to keep the plaster from sticking. You will need a **nail** for gouging lines on the hard plaster and **varnish** to keep the block printing paint from soaking into the printing block. You will also need an old **cooky sheet** and a **brayer** for rolling out the paint.

How to do it. After mixing the plaster, pour it into the cardboard mold. It will take about an hour for the plaster to harden. When it is completely solid, tear off the mold and draw your design on the plaster block. Then, use a nail to carve the lines, scratching out parts that are to be white, such as Santa's beard. Varnish the plaster block.

To make a print, first roll the brayer in the paint. Then roll the brayer over the block until it is completely coated with paint. Place a sheet of paper over the block, and holding it in place with one hand, firmly rub the surface with the other. Add more paint to the block as needed for the next print. When you have finished, use a cloth to clean the printing block.

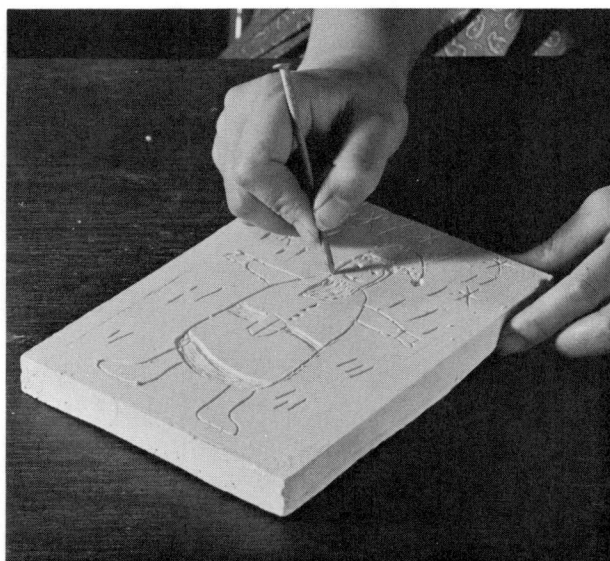

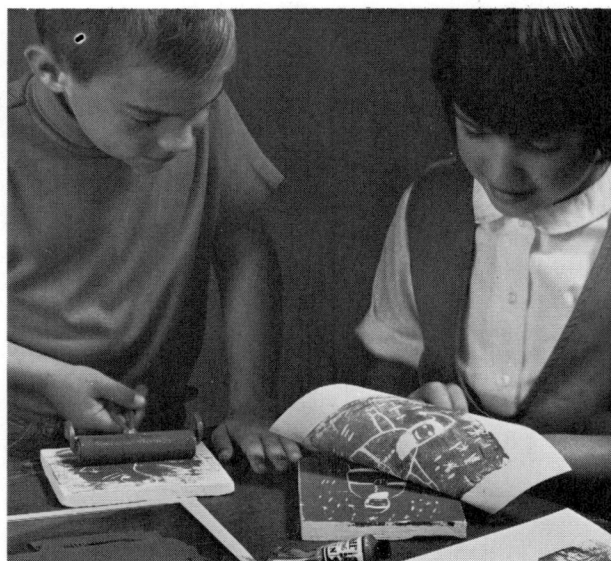

VACATION CRAFTS

SOUVENIR RUBBINGS • DECORATING ROCKS • LEAVES ON LETTERS
PRINTING WITH PODS • DISPLAYING LEAF COLLECTIONS • TEASEL FLOWERS
YULE LOG • WALKING STICKS • PINECONE OWL
DRIFTWOOD ZOO & SCULPTURE • WOVEN NATURE COLLECTION

Making souvenir rubbings

You know what a nice picture of Lincoln appears when you cover a penny with paper and scribble a crayon over it. This is called a rubbing. In much the same way, you can make rubbings of brass plates on the historical monuments you visit. You need lightweight **paper**—a roll of white shelf paper is handy—**masking tape,** and a piece of black **finishing wax** (any shoe repair shop has this kind of wax). You can also use the sides of a peeled, black crayon, but it won't work as well as the wax. To make the rubbing, tape a piece of paper over the brass plate and rub firmly with the wax until a picture appears.

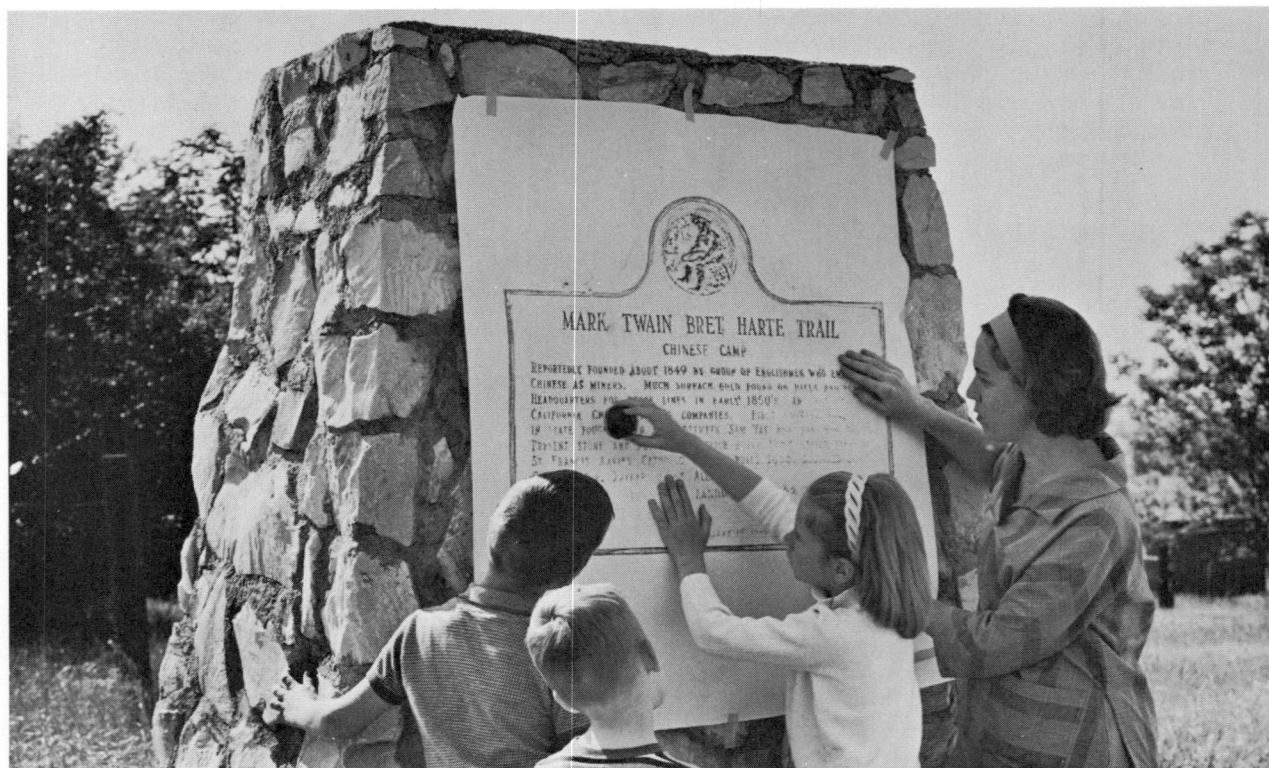

Rock dolls

Collecting rocks for little dolls is fun for girls and boys as well as their parents. Select rocks and pebbles that will look well together. Use the larger rocks for the bodies and the smaller rocks or pebbles for hands and feet. Fasten the pieces together using a fast-drying **glue**. Use **acrylic paints** to make features. In the picture at right, the girl doll has **yarn** hair and the parrot has **pipe cleaner** feet and collar.

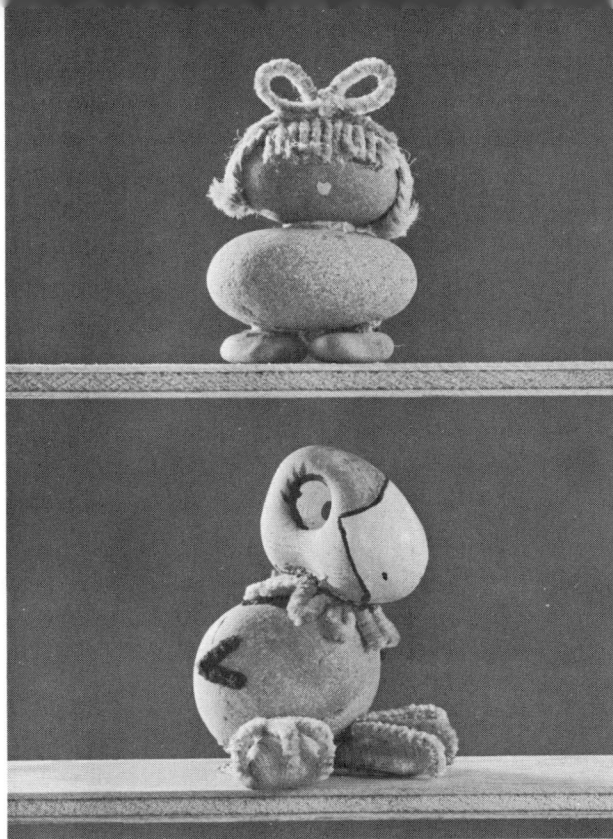

Painted faces on rocks

Funny faces, sad faces, animal faces, or monster faces—almost anything you like—are fun to paint on smooth rocks. On a visit to the desert, beach, or mountains, you can collect enough rocks in different sizes and shapes to make an unusual collection of faces. Spread **newspapers** over the work area. Then make sure that the rocks are clean and dry before you begin to paint. Use **acrylic paints** because they have bright colors and dry quickly. When you have finished painting, wash your brushes in water.

Leaf decorations for your letters

Little flowers and leaves can be collected to decorate writing paper for gifts or for your own use. Gather the **blossoms** and **leaves** in the fields or the mountains and press them between layers of **newspaper** until they are dry. Use a small brush to put dabs of **white glue** on the flowers and place them on the writing paper. Put the decorated paper between two pieces of **wax paper** and weight it down with a heavy **book** or **brick** so that it will not wrinkle while the glue is drying.

Printing with eucalyptus pods

Dry pods from the eucalyptus tree are excellent stamps to use for printing designs on note paper and envelopes. Some pods have a 5-point star design, others a 4-point design. First, gather the **pods.** So that they will be completely flat for printing, rub the design ends of the pods back and forth over a **file.** Then, using a small **brush,** coat the pod with thick **poster paint** and stamp it on the paper and envelopes. For each paint color, use a different pod.

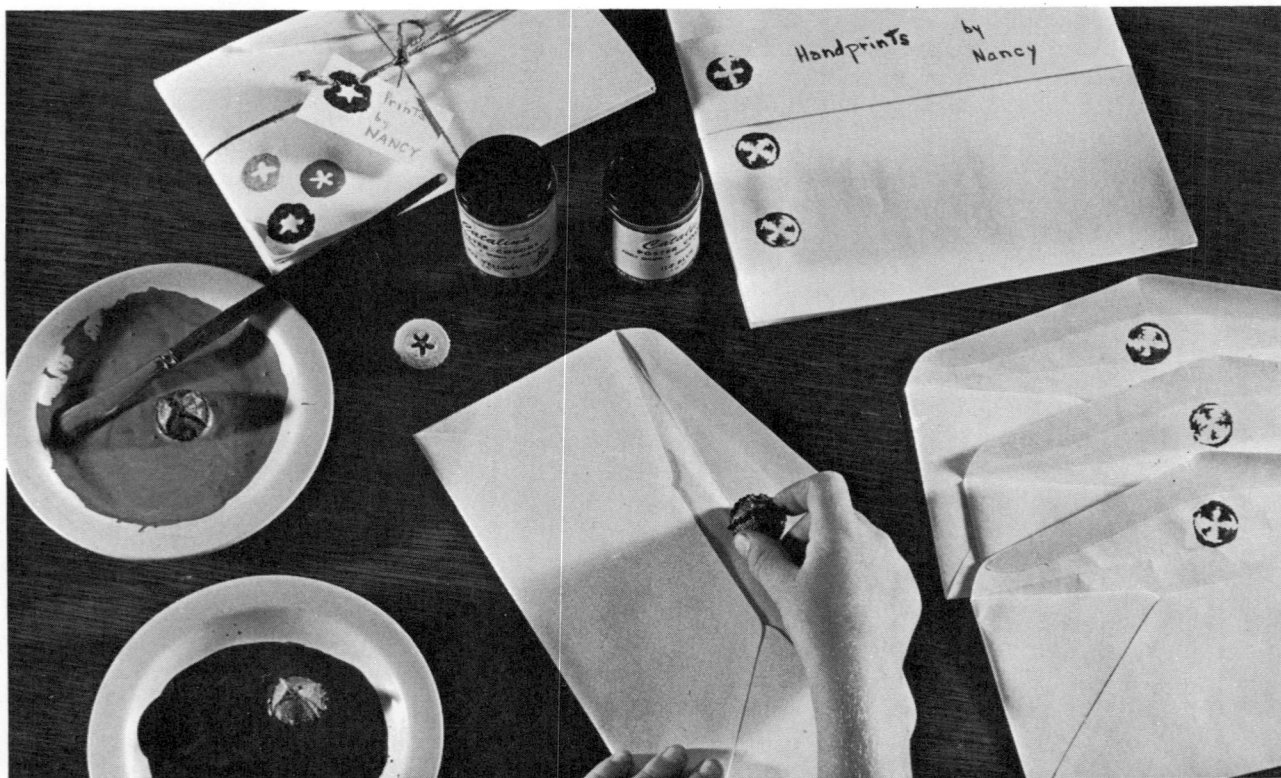

Sprigs on greeting cards

Fern fronds, evergreen tree sprigs, and snips of other plants that you have gathered on an outing in your own back yard, will make lively decorations for greeting cards.

What you need. Sprigs and **leaves** are mounted on **white index cards,** which in turn are mounted on folded, colored **construction paper.** You will also need transparent, sticky-backed **contact paper** (buy at a variety store) to cover and protect the decoration. Greetings are made with **felt pens** or **stick-down alphabet letters.**

How to make the cards. Place a leaf or sprig on an index card. If you want lettering on the card, put it on now. Then cut a piece of clear contact paper which is about a half inch larger on all sides than the index card. Peel off the backing of the contact paper and hold it in position over the decoration, sticky side down. (You cannot move it around once it is down.) Press the contact paper down firmly and fold the edges under the card. Mount the index card with glue on the folded construction paper.

Leaves on cork

One of the easiest ways of saving dried leaves is to mount them on a piece of cork (buy at a lumber yard). The eucalyptus leaves shown in the picture at left were first dried and pressed between the pages of an old telephone book. Then they were glued to the cork panel, each leaf overlapping the next.

Leaves on glass

If your mother tells you that it is alright, you can display a few dried flowers and leaves by gluing or taping them to a corner of your bedroom window. In the picture below, a spike of wheat makes the third side of a frame. A small, yellow butterfly has been added, too.

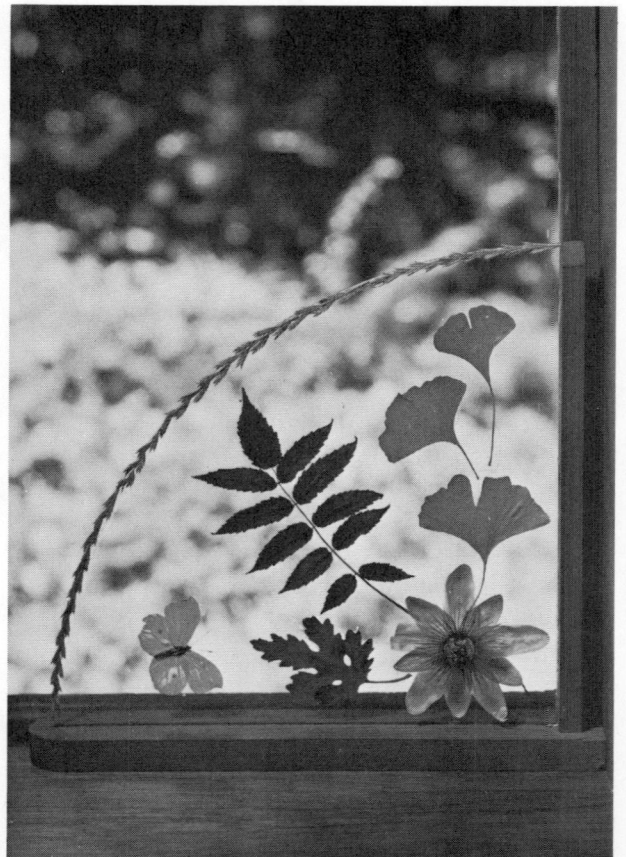

Flowers made from teasels

The flowers are made from dry teasel burs and seeds. A teasel is a weed that grows along the roadside and is ready to be picked at the end of summer. Handle with care because they have stickers.

Leaving the stems long, cut off the top half of the teasel bur with a **knife.** Paint dried sunflower or **pumpkin seeds** with bright **poster colors** and push them into the bur to look like flower petals. Decorate the center with a **stone** from an old piece of jewelry.

Display screen for leaves

A heavy paper screen, covered with squares of dark green and pale green **tissue paper,** makes a colorful background for displaying dried autumn leaves. Fold a 12-inch-wide and 20-inch-long **poster board** into four or five sections. Then divide each folded section into four equal parts and glue a piece of tissue paper over each section. Choose the most colorful dried leaves from your collection, brush the back of each one with **white glue,** and place them on the screen. For a glossy finish that will also keep the leaves from crumbling, brush on a coat of **polymer glaze** (buy at a craft shop).

A yule log for Christmas

On a trip to the mountains, you can very often find small logs to take home and save for decorating as yule logs at Christmas time.

What to use. Your **wagon** is a good workbench and will not only hold the log but also **evergreen branches** and **pine cones.** You will also need some **paraffin.**

How to do it. Ask your mother to melt the par-rafin and let it cool about a half hour before using. Then put it on the log in a big soft lump and press the ends of the evergreen branches into it. Add three or four pinecones and holly berries, too, if you have them.

Decorated walking sticks

There is something about hiking along a mountain path that makes you feel like carrying a walking stick. If you and your family like to hike, you will enjoy decorating a walking stick to take along. Find a nice, smooth **branch** or limb and make designs with **acrylic paints.** You can often paint faces using a knot as a nose (see the picture below).

A sleepy pinecone owl

Making a sleepy pinecone owl is a fast and easy project for young boys and girls who are away at camp. First, find the biggest and fattest pinecone you can. Then, using pieces of orange and black **felt** or **construction paper**, make eyes, a beak, and 4-toed feet. Attach them with **glue.**

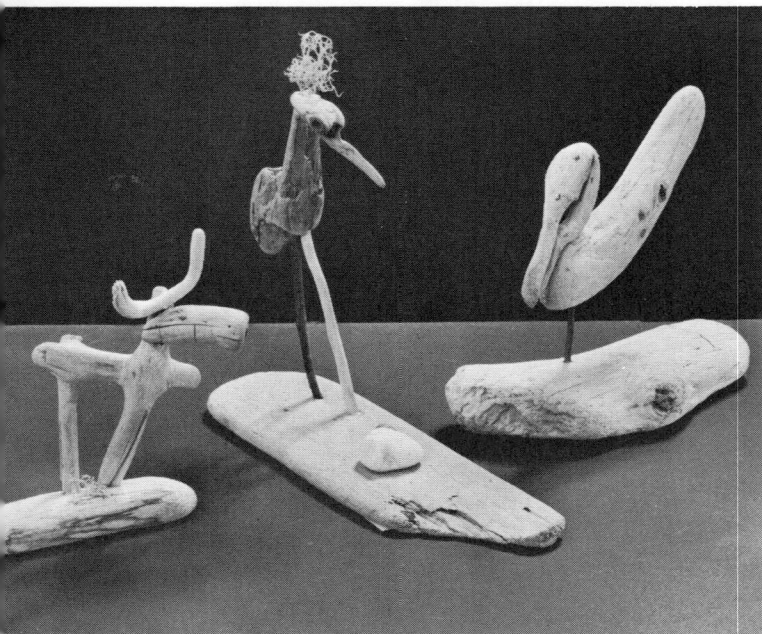

A zoo with driftwood animals

You can be sure that no one else in the world will have a zoo exactly like yours if the animals are made of driftwood. On your next visit to the beach, see how many interesting pieces of driftwood you can collect. Often the pieces that you find will already look just like an animal (for example, the figure on the right in the picture at left looks like a seagull). Some pieces of driftwood will need a little dressing up to make them look like animals. Moss was used to make a topknot for the bird in the center of the picture and a smooth, curved stick was used for the deer's antlers.

Natural driftwood sculpture

The odd-shaped piece of gray driftwood in the picture below was found with two tiny shells already half buried in a crack. Small, shiny beach pebbles were added and glued into little holes carved with a knife. The duck is made from three pieces of driftwood glued together.

A woven nature collection

Weaving a collection of leaves, pods, and twigs through a piece of burlap is an excellent craft project for a group at day camp. You need a piece of **burlap** which is about 7 inches wide and 14 inches long. You will also need **thumbtacks** for attaching the burlap to a heavy **stick** for hanging. To make this wall hanging, follow these directions.

Row 1: Pull out 12 threads across the piece of burlap. Weave 3 sticks and 3 long foxtail weeds in and out of the up-and-down threads. Glue on a dried pod.

Row 2: Weave a stiff black plastic cord across the burlap and glue on 5 dried pods about a half inch apart.

Row 3: Pull out 10 threads and weave in two stiff, leathery leaves.

Row 4: Pull out 15 threads and weave in three sticks which are covered with bark.

Row 5: Weave in the stem of a dried thistle.

Row 6: Pull out 15 threads and weave in straw from an old broom.

Row 7: Pull out 15 threads and weave in a piece of heavy bark.

CRAFTS FROM ODDS AND ENDS

PAPER BAG PUPPETS & TURKEY • PAPER PLATE MUSIC
PAPER PLATE ELEPHANT MASK • FUNNY EYES
EGG CARTON WITCHES & CANDLEHOLDER
"BOO" MASK • LONG TAPE GREETING CARDS • NEWSPAPER NECKLACE
OLD-FASHIONED VALENTINES • EASTER EGGS • MOBILE WITH WALNUT BOATS
WALKING WALNUT ANIMALS • PAPER FLOWERS • TIN CAN LANTERNS
DOUBLE CANDLES • MEXICAN YARN ORNAMENTS • WAX PAPER MOBILE
WIRE JEWELRY • DECORATED BOTTLES • TOOTHPICK STARS

Paper bag puppets

A den of Cub Scouts can have a wonderful time making paper bag puppets at one meeting and giving a puppet show the next. Cut the faces from colored **construction paper** and **glue** each one to the bottom of a bag.

Paper bag turkey

This big, plump turkey makes a colorful Thanksgiving decoration. It is made from a brown **paper bag** and colored **construction paper.** Using the biggest bag you can find, stuff it with crumpled **newspapers,** tie it closed with a **string,** and fan out the top. Cut 7 or 8 fringed feathers from colored construction paper and **glue** them to the top of the bag. Following the pattern below, cut out and fold the turkey's head. Glue the two flaps to the bottom of the bag. Then cut out and glue the feet in place. Use **poster paint** to make the eyes and feathers.

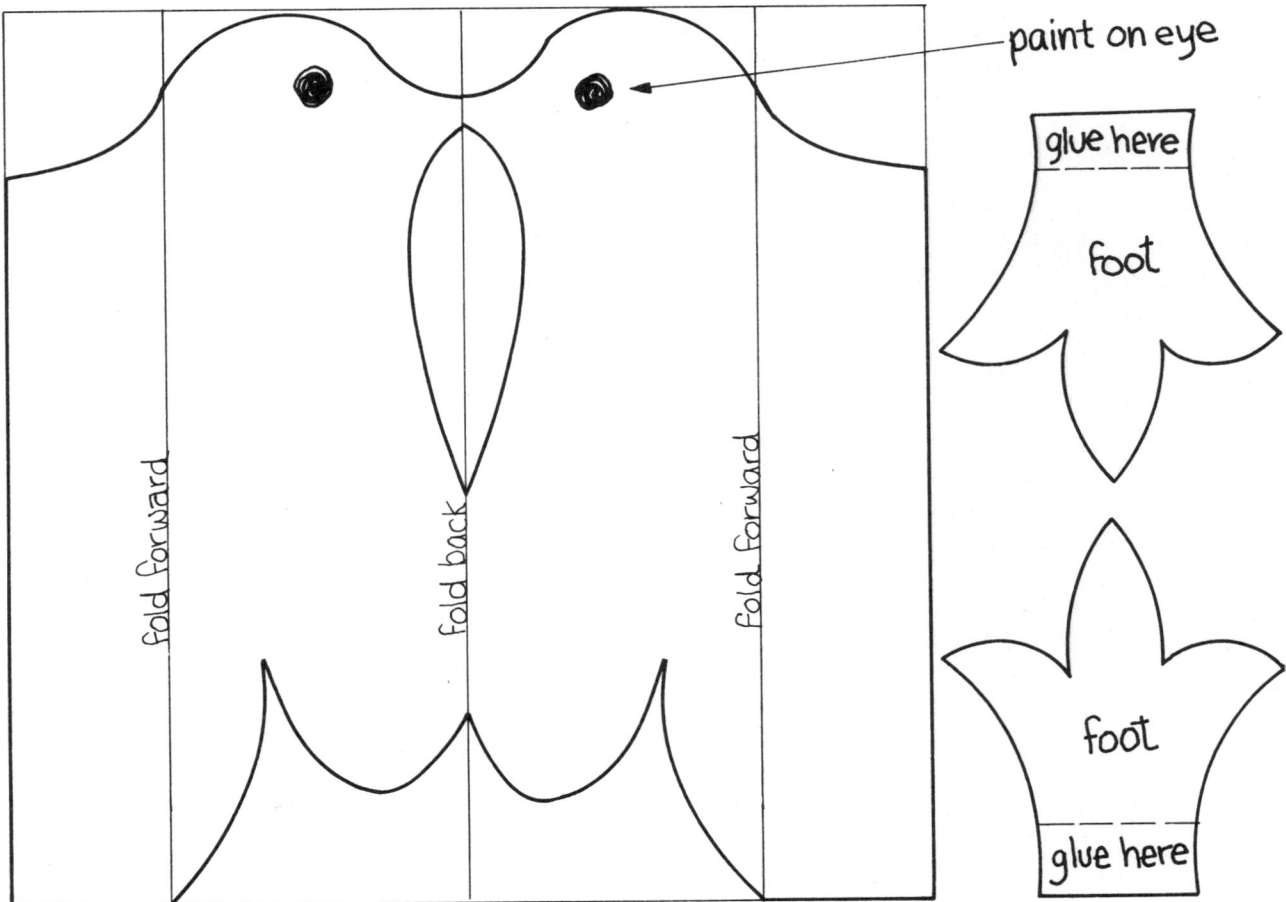

paint on eye

Fold Forward

Fold back

Fold Forward

glue here

foot

foot

glue here

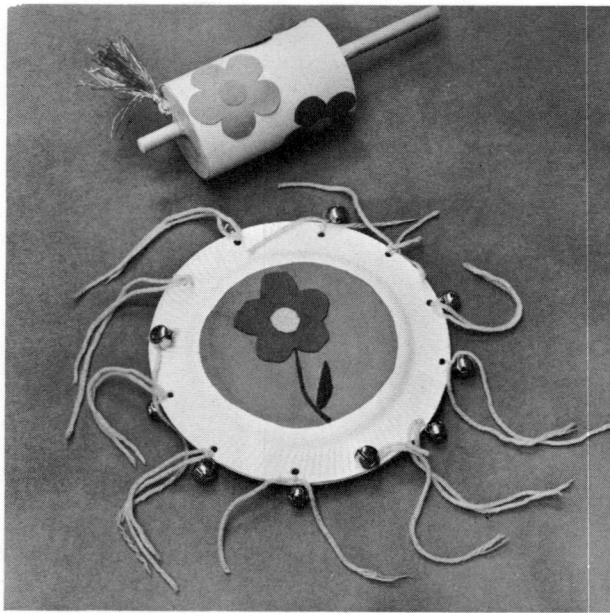

Music with paper plates and cartons

You can quickly make this easy tambourine and maraca using **paper plates** and a **salt carton**. To make the maraca, first put a few **beans** into an empty salt carton (for sound), **tape** it shut. Cover carton with **paper** and make a hole in the top and bottom. For the handle, push a **dowel** through these holes. Add cut out paper flowers and a **tassel**. To make the tambourine, hold the faces of the two paper plates together and punch holes around the edges. Using a length of **yarn**, tie a **bell** at each hole. **Glue** flower decorations to the front and back.

Elephant mask and funny eyes

This boy and girl are wearing masks that can be made quickly and easily. The funny eyes are made from two cups cut from an **egg carton** and a long **ribbon**. Decorate the egg cups with **poster paint** and **staple** them to the ribbon. The elephant mask is like the one shown on the cover of this book. It is made from a **paper plate**, with ears and tusks cut out from **construction paper** and glued in place. The squirmy trunk is made from long strips of paper. Following the drawing below, place two strips of paper across another strip. Fold under A, fold over B, C, and D. Continue folding C and D up and over until the trunk is the length you want.

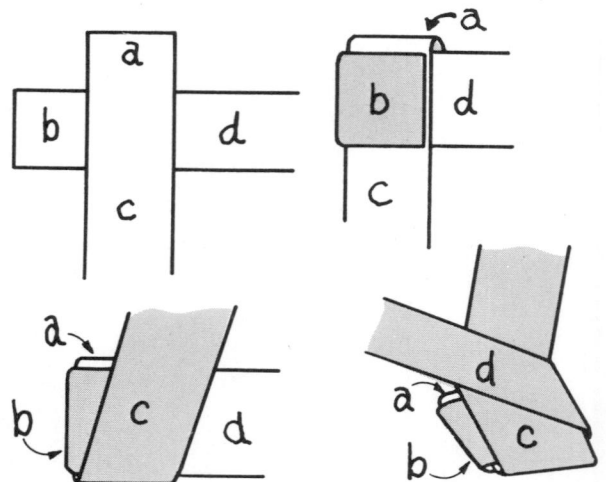

Egg carton candleholder

Camp Fire Girls are lighting candles for a ceremonial (a meeting when awards are given). They made the candleholder from an **egg carton** turned upside down and painted a bright green with **poster paint**. They also painted yellow and pink flowers, and added real ivy leaves and candles.

Egg carton witch faces

A windowful of witches on Halloween would be a very scary sight. To make the witches you will need several **egg cartons**. One carton will make three witches, so start saving them early in October. For each witch, cut a 4-cup section from the carton. Using **black paper,** cut out a high, pointed hat and **glue** it to the top edge. Make big round eyes and a turned down mouth using **poster paint** or crayons. Tie a **thread** to the top of each hat and hang the witches in a window.

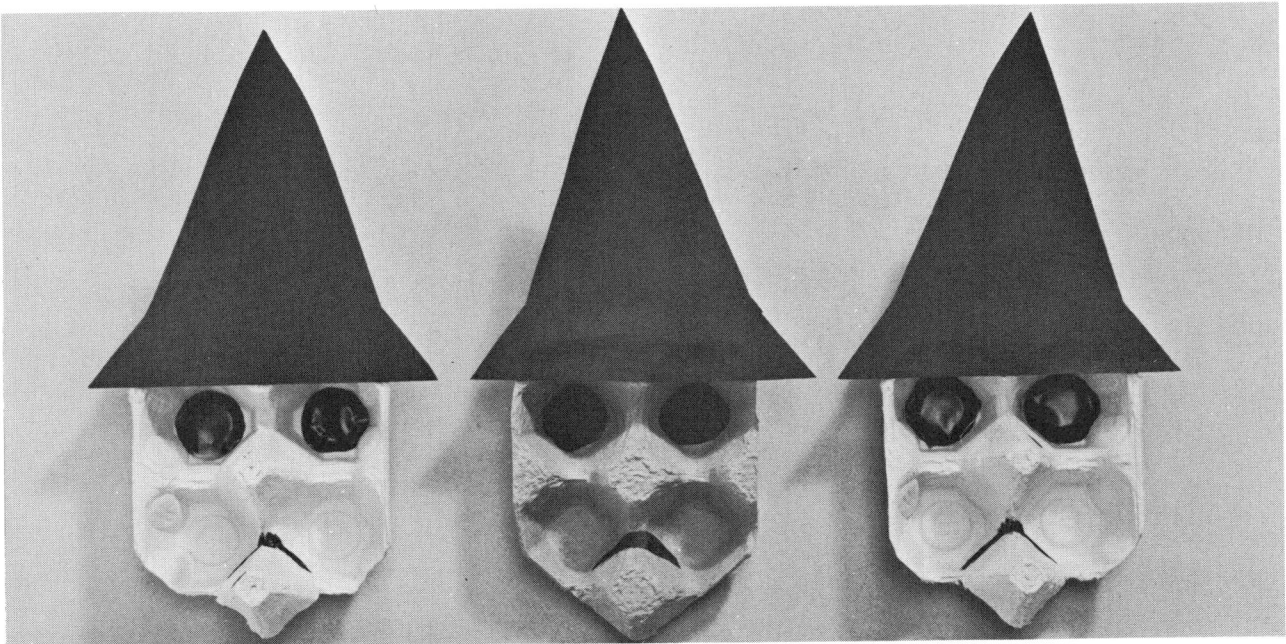

A mask that says "BOO"

These Halloween glasses that say "BOO" can be used by small children who do not want to wear a mask the whole evening. When you want to be scary, peek through the two O's. On heavy **colored paper** print the word "BOO" in big, thick letters. Be sure the letters join at some point. Cut out the word and **glue** it to a **dowel** or a thin stick. Add long strips of colored paper at the top.

Santa Claus candy box

This Santa Claus candy box not only holds a supply of gumdrops, but it also makes a bright Christmas decoration. You can make it from a small round **carton** that has a lid. For the beard, glue a large piece of **cotton** to the lower part of the carton. Use a little roll of cotton for the mustache. To the lid, glue a red **crepe paper** cap, twisted into a peak. Add a cotton **tassel**, and draw in the eyes and nose with colored **crayons**.

Greeting cards by the foot

A roll of white paper adding machine tape will make a dozen greeting cards several feet long. The tape costs about thirty cents at a stationery store. First, decide what you want to say on the card and then go through old **magazines** to find printing and pictures that you can use to tell the story. Especially look for bright colored pictures. After you have pasted the words and pictures to the tape, roll it up, and tie it with a **ribbon**. Shown here is a get-well card, which begins, "Eye here you're in the horse-pital, so bee an angel and get well".

A necklace of newspaper beads

Using long triangles of newspaper, you can make paper beads that can be strung on **yarn** or a **leather thong**. Make the triangles as long as the width of the newspaper page with the wide ends about 2 inches across. Starting with the wide ends, wrap the triangles around a **knitting needle**. **Glue** the small ends so the beads won't unwind. Slip the beads off the knitting needle and string them on a piece of yarn, using a large sewing needle.

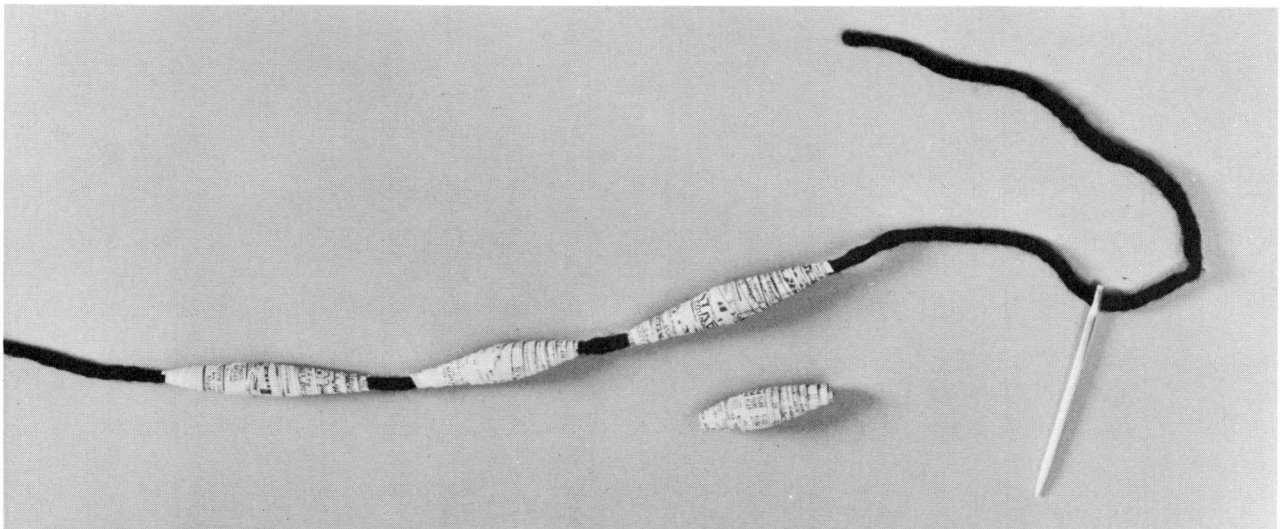

Old-fashioned valentines

To give some valentines an old-fashioned look, decorate them with lacy paper **doilies** and **fancy paper.** Choose heavy **construction paper** or stiff watercolor paper for your cards, but do not cut the paper until you know the size envelopes you will use. Then collect unusual gift wrapping papers and cut out different designs to be used with the pieces of doilies. Arrange the designs on the cards and glue with **rubber cement.**

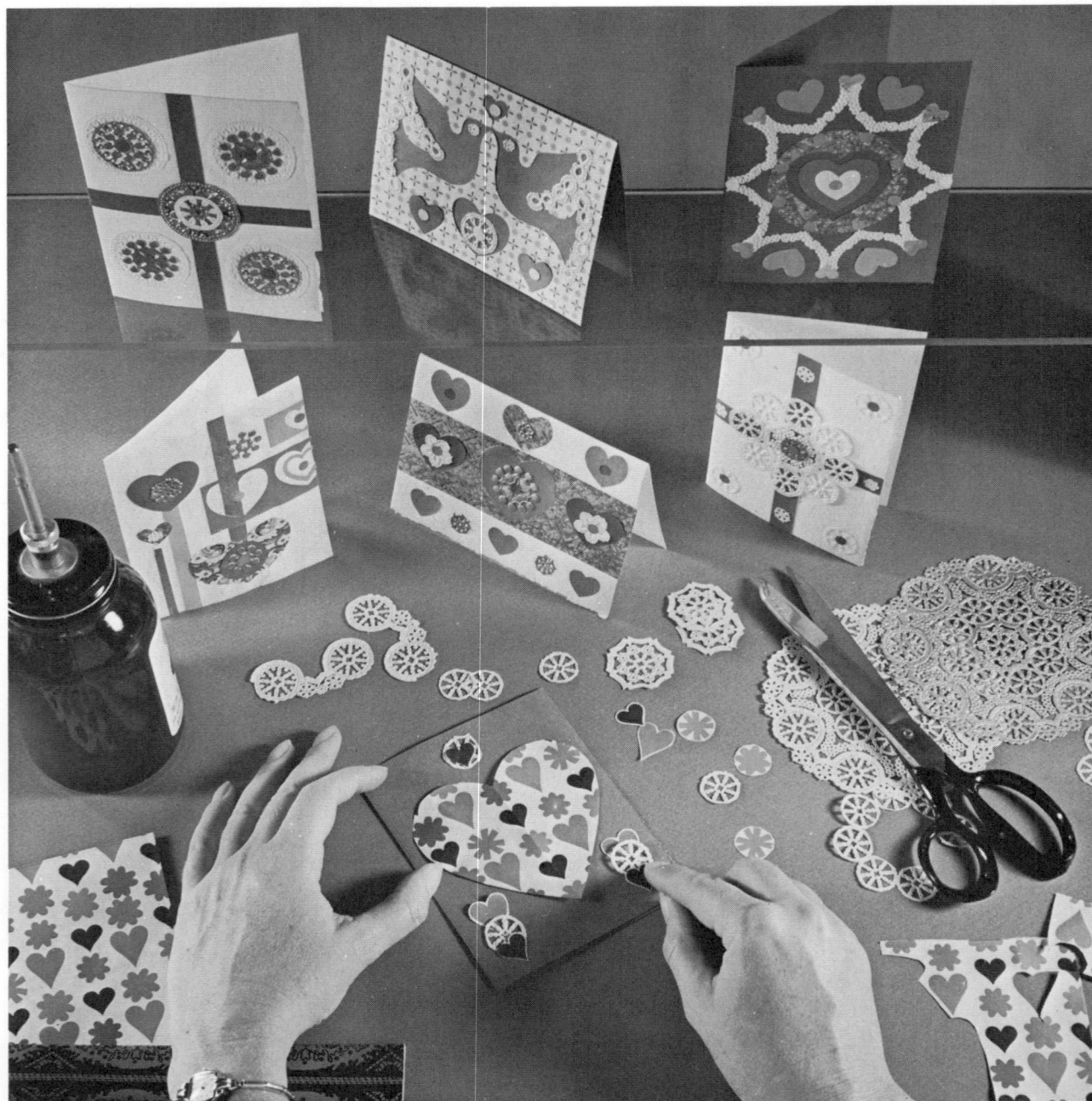

Blowing eggs for Easter

The best thing about making Easter eggs from blown eggs is that you can keep them from year to year. You need fresh **eggs** and a big **needle**. Begin by shaking the egg. This will help to loosen the inside of the egg so that it will be easier to blow. Using the needle, carefully make a hole at one end of the egg and another one a bit larger at the other end. Hold the egg over a bowl and blow gently into the smaller hole until the yolk and white are completely out. Wash the shell and stand it on end to dry. After blowing several eggs, start to decorate. In the picture below, some of the egg shells were first colored with a regular **Easter egg dye.** Scraps of **paper, yarn, cloth, beads,** and **feathers** were then used as decorations. A **felt marking pen** was used to draw features.

Mobile with walnut boats

The five little boats that sail around on this mobile are made from halves of **walnut shells.** The boats hang from two 12-inch **sticks** that have been crossed and tied at the center joint. Carefully crack the walnuts in two and take out the meat. **Glue** in a little piece of hard plastic **foam** or **balsa wood.** Into this base, glue a **toothpick** which has a tiny paper sail attached. Tie threads to the toothpick tops and hang the boats from the crosspiece.

Walking walnut animals

These walnut animals can scamper quickly down a smooth slope—the turtle moves as fast as the mouse. Halves of **walnut shells** are used for the bodies with bits of **felt** attached for eyes, head, feet, and tail. The mouse whiskers are pieces of **straw** from a broom. Use **white glue** for attaching all decorations. When the animals are finished, put a **marble** under each one and watch them scramble down a slanting book or board.

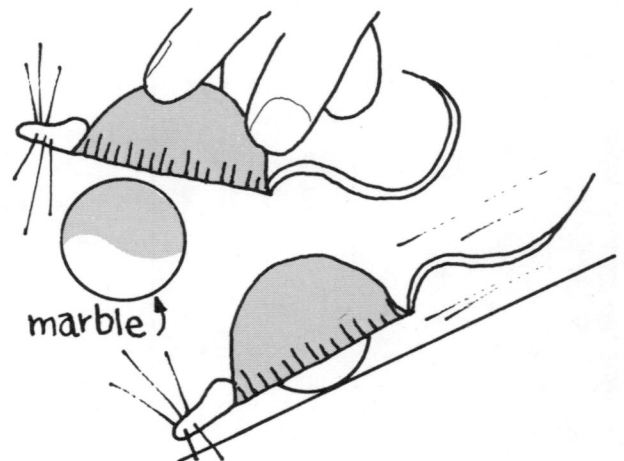

marble

Paper flowers in an orange juice can

An empty, frozen orange juice can filled with a bunch of paper flowers makes a pretty kitchen decoration to give your mother.

What to use. Sticky backed **contact paper** covers the **orange juice can** and is also used to make the flowers. Choose a printed paper and a plain one. Eight-inch pieces of thin, **soft wire** are used for the flower stems that are stuck into **clay**. Colored **tissue paper** is crumpled into the top of the can.

How to do it. After tracing the flower pattern below on the contact paper, cut out two times as many flower outlines as you want to use. Peel off the backing on one flower and lay a wire on the sticky side as shown in the drawing. Then, leaving the backing on a second flower, carefully place it over the sticky side of the first flower and press it down firmly. This makes a stiff-petaled blossom that can be curved. Cover the orange juice can with contact paper and stick the wire ends of the flowers into a piece of clay in the bottom of the can. When the flowers are arranged, loosely fill the can with crumpled tissue paper.

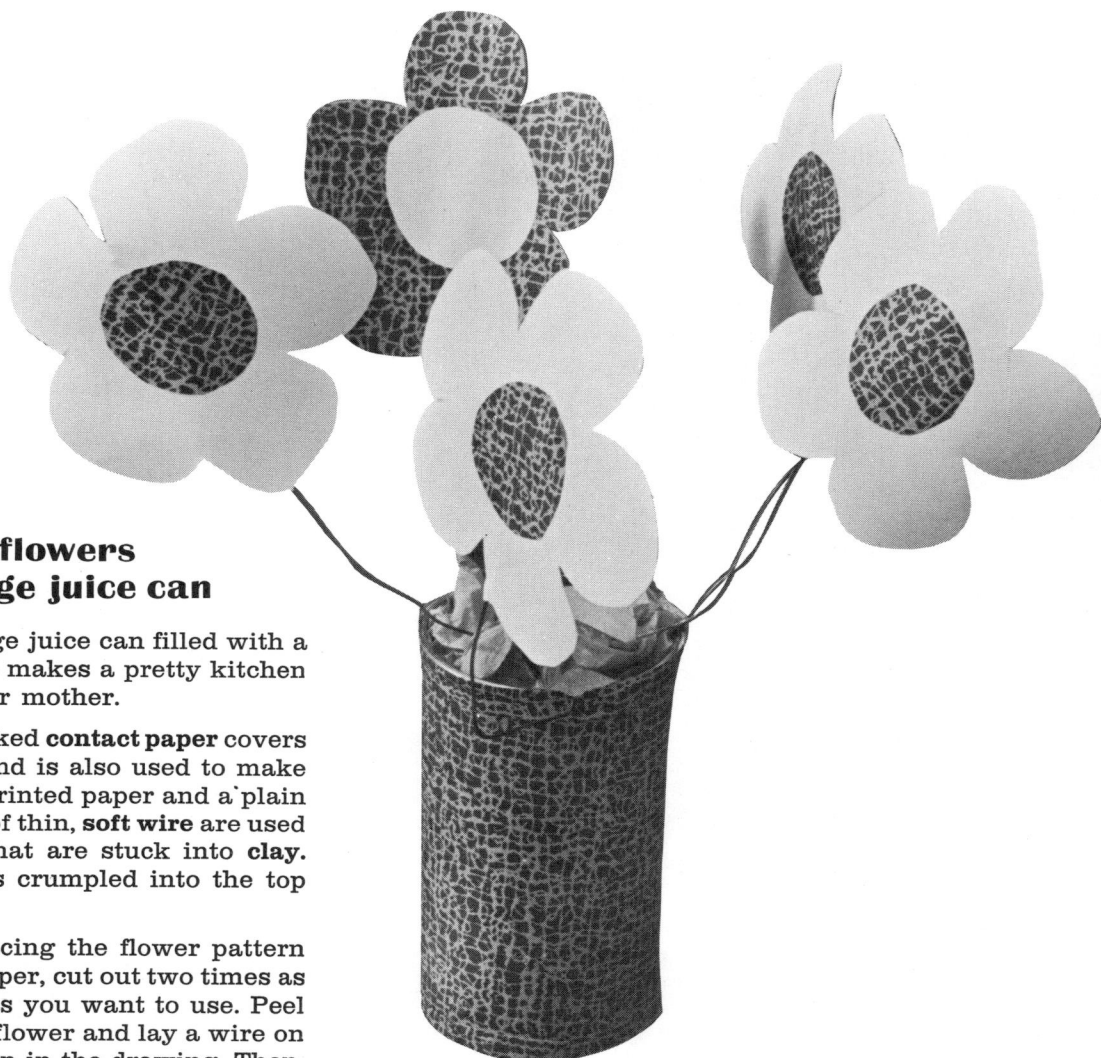

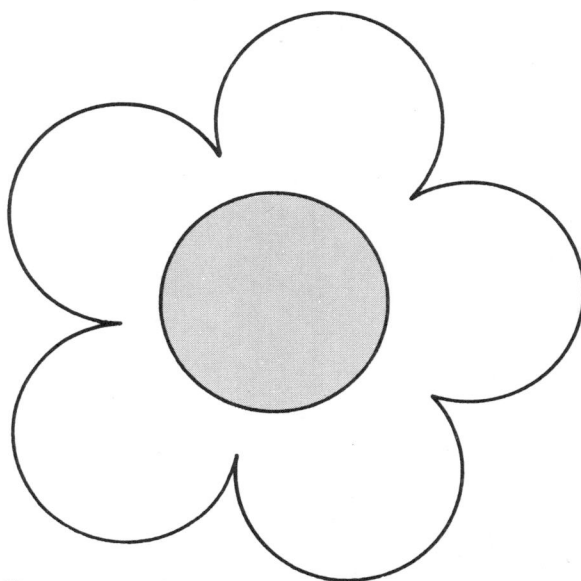

peel off backing

flower cut out with backing still on

wire

Tin can lanterns

Here is a clever way to make Christmas lanterns out of tin cans. With some grown-up help, it is an excellent craft for a group of Scouts.

How to make them. You can use any size **tin can,** from dog food to fruit juice size. Fill each can with **water** to 1/4 inch below the rim and place it in the freezer for about two days, until the ice is very hard. Then cut a piece of heavy **paper** big enough to fit around the can and draw your design. Fasten the pattern around the can with **cloth tape** or masking tape. Place the can on an old, folded **towel.** Using a **hammer** and a **nail,** punch holes into the can along the lines of your design. If the ice starts to melt before you have finished, put it in the freezer, paper and all, and start on another lantern.

Lacy, double candles

Pretty and lacy, these two candles are made using a ready-made candle, little ice cubes, and melted paraffin. You will need some grown-up help because the paraffin must be melted over a flame and it burns **very** easily.

How to make them. Ahead of time, fill an **ice cube tray** only half full and put it in the freezer. Then make a **cardboard mold** from an oatmeal or salt box, cutting the top off to the size you want. Coat the inside of the mold with **cooking oil**. Choose a ready-made **candle** which is a little higher than the mold and place it in the center of the mold. Pour an inch of **melted parrafin** around the base of the candle to hold it in place. Using the small ice cubes that you have made earlier, gently drop in a layer of ice. Cover it with hot wax to which you have added shavings of **crayons** a different color from the wick candle. Repeat these layers until the mold is filled. Let the wax harden overnight and tear away the mold.

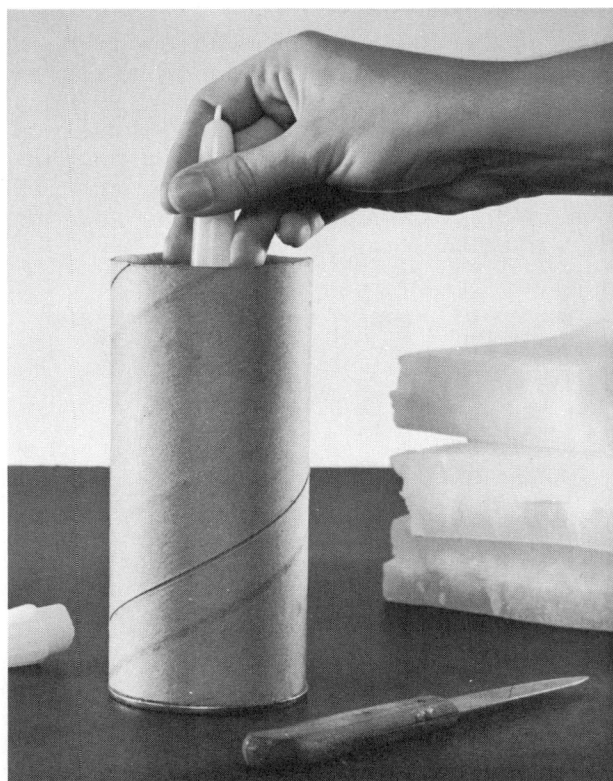

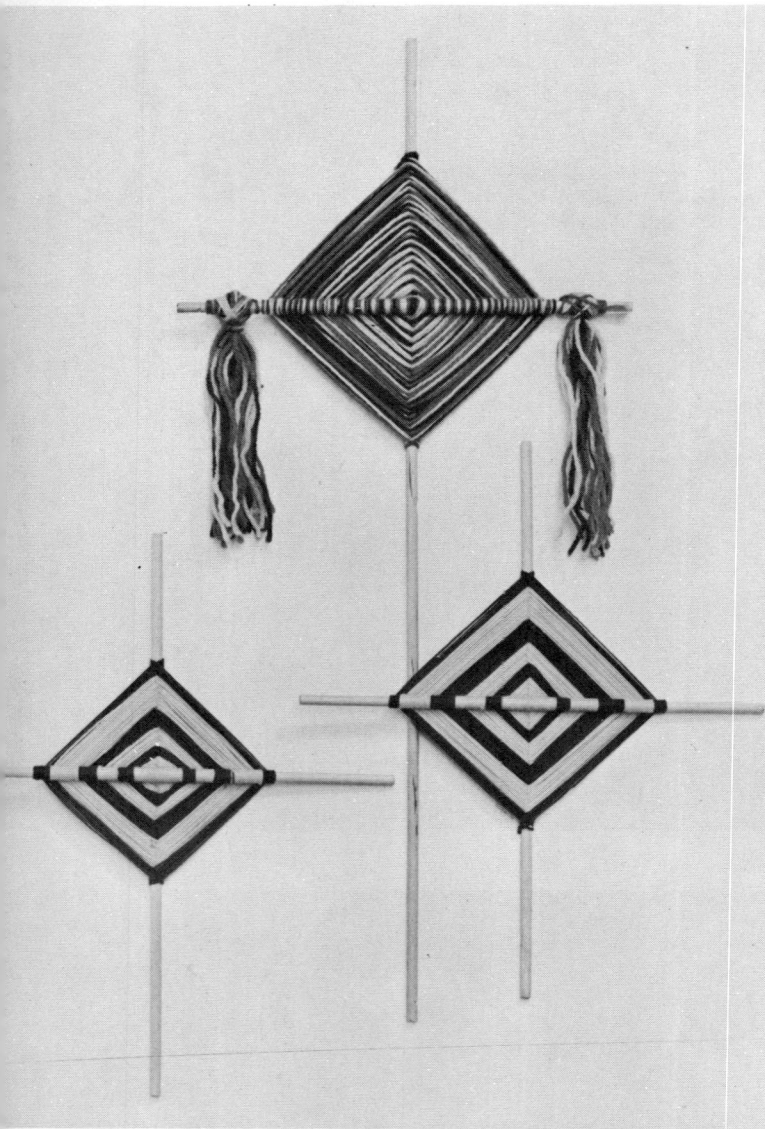

Mexican yarn ornaments

In Mexico, these ornaments are called **ojo de Dios,** which means "eye of God" in Spanish. You can make one quickly using two sticks and a ball of yarn. Ojos look well with the lanterns shown on page 90.

How to make an ojo. As shown in the pictures below, cross two sticks, fasten them together with **white glue.** At the center joint, loop the **yarn** over both arms several times to make it firm (see picture No. 1). Next, wrap the yarn once around each arm, one arm after the other (see picture No. 2). Continue until the ojo is the right size (see picture No. 3).

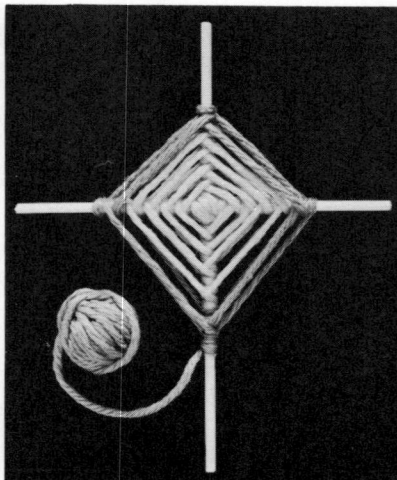

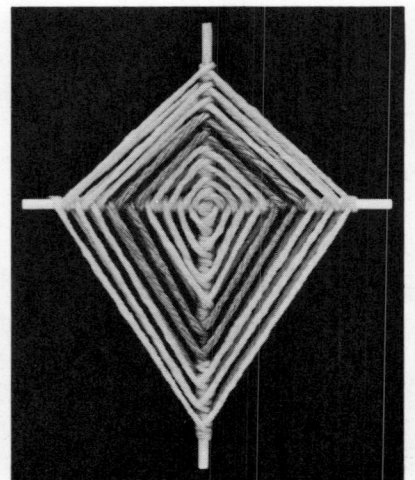

A wax paper mobile

These bright butterflies sparkle like jewels in the sunlight. **Wax paper,** tiny scraps of colored **tissue paper, thread,** a **stick,** and a warm **iron** are all you need to make them. Tear off two pieces of wax paper each a foot long. On one, arrange scraps of tissue paper in shapes to look like butterflies. Carefully place the other piece of wax paper over them and gently press with a warm iron. This will seal the design between the wax papers. Leaving about a quarter inch around each design, cut out the butterflies. Tie them by threads to a small stick.

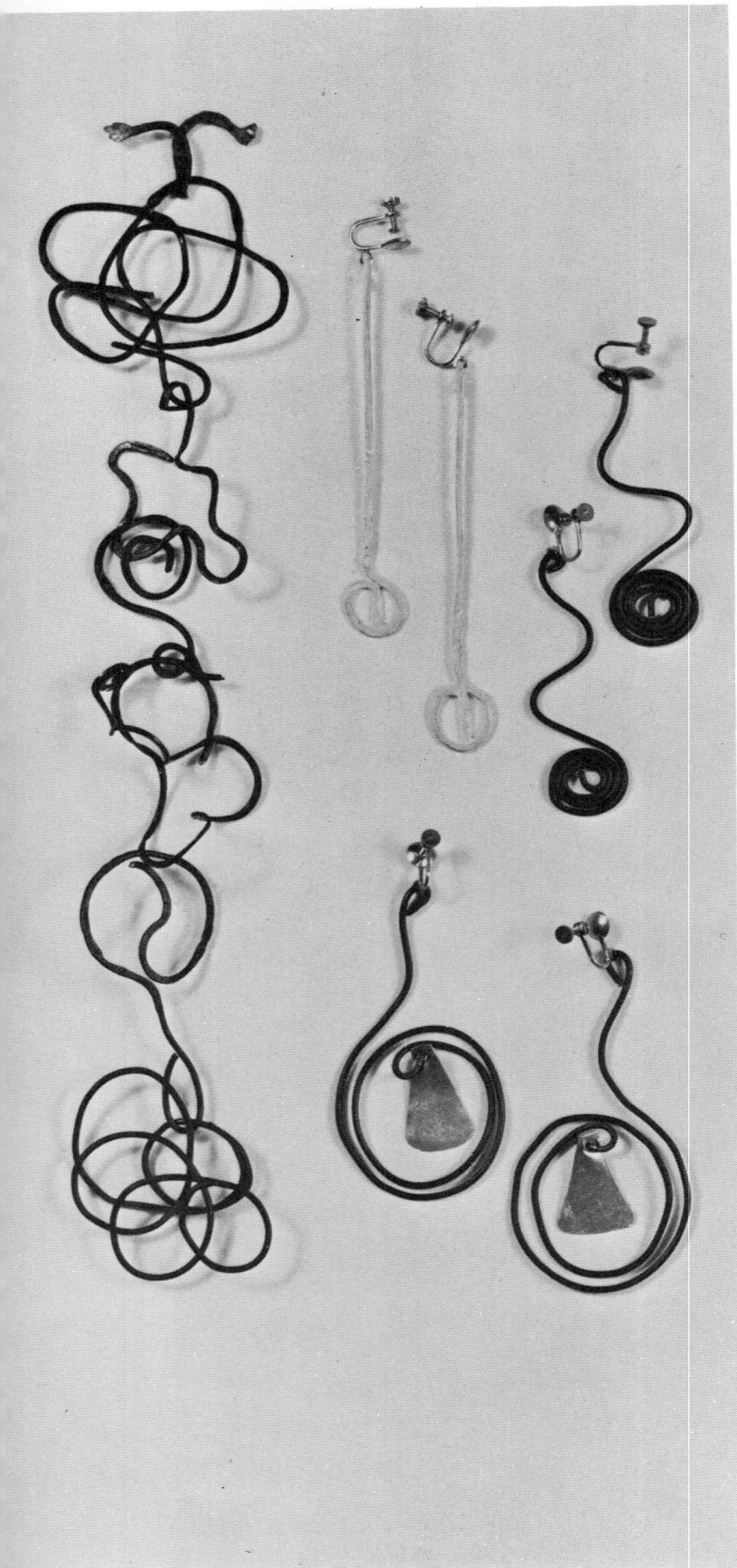

Wire jewelry or decorations

Soft wire, hammered flat and then twisted into swirls and kinks, makes unusual jewelry to give a grown-up sister. You can also twist the wire into a number of shapes, loop them together and hang them up for decorations.

What to use. Use any kind of thin, soft **wire** that can be hammered easily. You also need a **hammer** and a pair of **wire cutting pliers.** A piece of **metal** makes a good surface for hammering the wire (an old hinge like the one shown in the picture at right is handy). Buy **bases for earrings** at a dime store or hobby shop.

How to do it. It is a good idea to work outdoors where you can place the piece of metal on a block of wood. Using the wire cutters, snip off the length of wire you need. Put the wire on the metal and flatten it with the hammer. Then bend it into the shape you want.

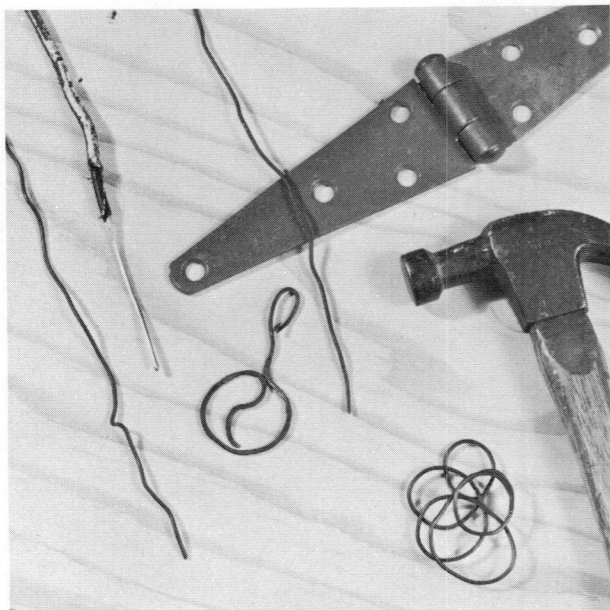

Decorated glass and plastic bottles

Something useful and attractive can be created from most empty bottles that are usually thrown away. The vitamin bottles in the picture are decorated with scraps of colored **tissue paper** and filled with **rice** and **barley**. The string-wrapped container was made by using a **craft knife** to cut the top off a plastic oil bottle. The outside was covered with **white glue** and then wrapped with **heavy twine**.

Bright-colored stars made of toothpicks

Bright stars like these can be made from **toothpicks, white glue, cardboard,** and **gold paint.** On cardboard, draw a cross about 6 inches long with 1-inch-wide arms. Brush on a coat of glue and place toothpicks across the design as the drawing shows. Then glue toothpicks to the arms. Finally, add another cross of toothpicks over the first one.

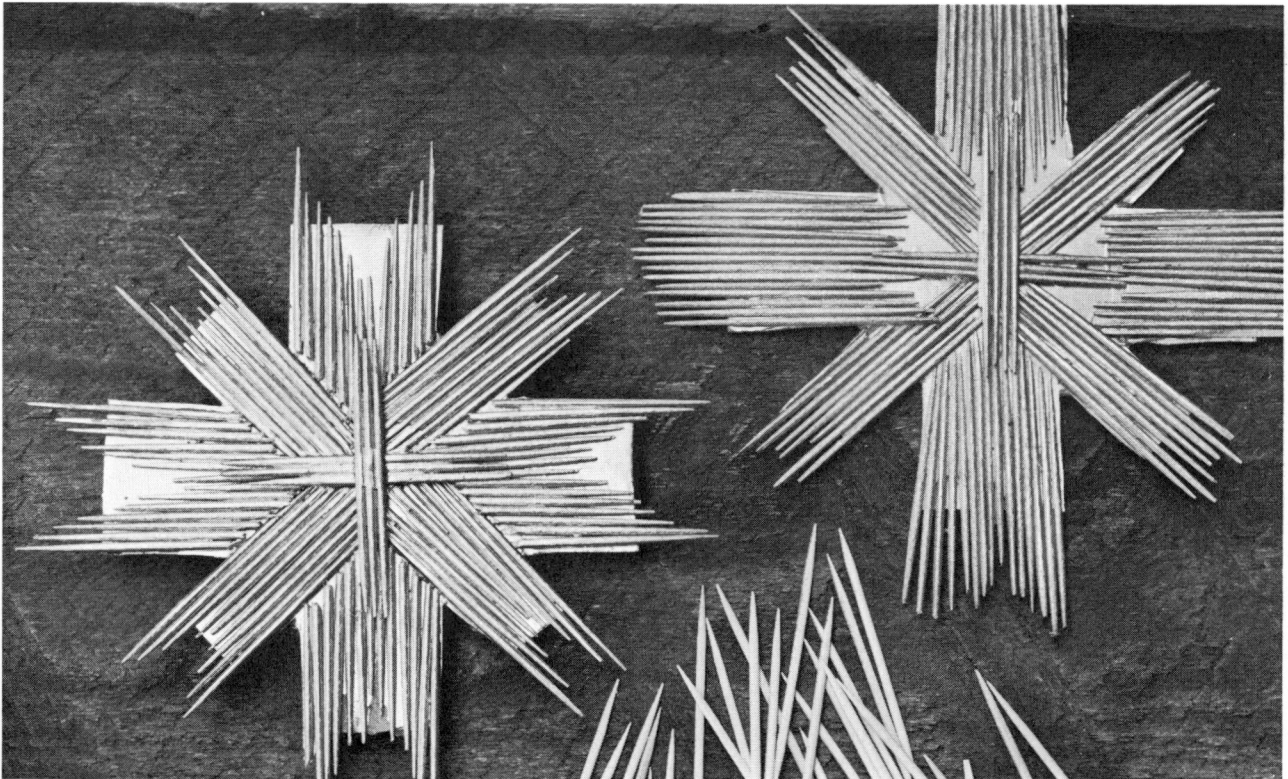

PHOTOGRAPHERS

Glenn M. Christiansen: pages 73, 76, 87. **Robert Cox:** pages 14, 18 (bottom), 21, 33, 35 (top), 38, 39, (top), 41 (top), 44 (top right), 46, 47, 48, 56, 57 (top), 58, 59, 60, 61, 63 (right), 64, 65 (top), 67, 69 (top), 75 (top), 77, 78, 81, 82, 83, 84, 85, 88, 89, 92 (top), 93, 94, 95. **Virginia Davidson:** page 68. **Jack McDowell:** pages 6, 7, 10, 11, 12 (left), 13, 15 (top), 17, 20 (top left and bottom), 23, 24, 25, 26, 27, 30, 35 (bottom), 36 (right), 37, 39, 41 (bottom), 42 (bottom), 43, 49, 50 (top), 51 (bottom), 63 (left), 79, 80. **Tom Riley:** page 51 (top). **Blair Stapp:** pages 54, 55. **Darrow M. Watt:** pages 12 (right), 15 (bottom), 16, 18 (top), 20 (top right), 29, 30, 32, 34, 36 (left), 44 (top left and bottom), 45, 50 (bottom), 52, 53, 57 (bottom), 62, 65 (bottom), 66, 69 (bottom), 70, 71, 72, 74, 75 (bottom), 86, 90, 91 (bottom), 92 (bottom). **George Woo:** page 91 (top).